A Wife's Guide to **Removing the But** and Embracing Your Husband's Personality as a Gift

DR. ROBERT PYLES

Copyright © 2020 Robert B. Pyles

All rights reserved. No part of this book may be reproduced or transmitted in any form or by any means without written permission from the author.

I Love My Husband But
ISBN: 978-1-952327-15-5
Library of Congress Control Number: pending

Dedication

To my beautiful wife, Betty, thank you for loving me without the "buts." Together we've built the marriage of our dreams—34 years and counting.

Contents

Foreword 5
Before You Begin Reading 7
Happily Ever After 13
From Dating to Distance 23
Purpose Over Problems 29
Two Personalities One Marriage 37
Honesty Heals 61
Complex Issues With Simple Solutions 75
Loving Your Husband Without the But 129
Next Steps 135

Foreword

God loves marriage, and He designed it for husbands and wives to love it as well. I believe marriage is one of the most fulfilling and rewarding relationships a man and woman can experience here on earth. Having been married over four decades, I know the gift of marrying the one God had in mind before this world began. I know what it means to grow together and to grow up together; because of this, I know how powerful a resource like this book is to a healthy marriage.

In his companion books, I Love My Wife, But and I Love My Husband, But — Pastor Pyles provides a classical compilation of truths. No matter what stage of marriage you are in, both husband and wife can grow from this work. By entering this experience with an open heart, you will discover and recover God's purpose for your union. We often forget that understanding is a core longing of every individual, especially in marriage. Pastor Pyles offers critical insights into understanding how you and your mate are uniquely wired and handknit together by God. He then challenges both husband and wife to love the personality traits that may have caused a "but" somewhere in your love walk with your mate.

For over twenty years, Pastor Pyles has been a son and a protégé of mine. I've watched his life as an innovator, trailblazer, and visionary champion of faith for his family and his community. As you read, I promise you will also grow. If you allow the anointing on this book to saturate your marital union, you will be thankful you've discovered this treasure.

My Highest Regards,

E L Warren, Ph.D
Bishop, Cathedral Of Worship
President, E L Warren Min Int
Presiding Prelate I.N.A.M
Member, Illinois State Police Merit Board
Chairman, Center for Family Preservation
Treasure International Communion Of Charismatic Churches

Before You Begin Reading

Did you know the very thing you loved about your husband, that drew you to him, that mesmerized you and captivated your attention could become the same thing you despise about him years later? Think about it, for the wife that married the husband that gives her everything she wants. He's easy to please, allows her to have her way, and showers her with "yes" whenever there's a question. He is quick to say, "you decide, whatever you want to do is fine with me." Initially, this amazing man that gives her everything she wants and needs while allowing her to lead the way is exactly what she's always wanted. Until the marriage grows and it's time to make decisions.

The qualities that she once adored now becomes a thorn in her side because guess what – he won't make a decision. Not because he can't, but because it's not how he's wired. He wasn't wired that way from the beginning. However, because decision making wasn't something she needed (or wanted) him to do from the beginning, he wasn't accustomed to doing it. He never changed, he still provides the "yes, honey, whatever you want – however, you want to do it." The difference is now she is full of frustration because he won't make a decision! She finds herself saying things like:

- I always have to plan the vacation…
- If I don't do it, it won't be done…
- He makes me handle everything …

How is it that the things she once loved so much have become vices in their relationship? In this book, "I Love My Husband, But" and the companion – "I Love My Wife, But" I will highlight how strengths and opportunities in relationships are based on our wiring and personality. The husband in this relationship isn't wired to be the heavy, his personality is more than likely laid back, easy-going, and when he says "it's up to you" he really means it. I am confident there is a woman who just read that scenario, and they have already inserted her husband into that example as a perfect fit.

Wives, trust me, I address the husbands the same way in the companion book. I encourage to read it and hear what I say to them after you've received what I'm sharing with you. I wrote this to offer you a practical perspective on removing the but out of your marriage and embrace your husband's personality as a gift. He is still the man you fell in love with and the man you love.

I realized that even loving couples who have been married for decades were yet struggling with some of the same issues as younger couples and the newly married. Challenges for those that have been married for decades were the same challenges causing the newlyweds to walk away from their marriage. It's all centered around personality. My gift to understand personality and how people are wired has already been a blessing in various industries. I've helped young and old, business owners and employees, men and women, understand their personality and identify areas of opportunity and maximize areas of strength.

This time, I'm writing to those that are married, have been married, and desire to become married. Couples are the backbone of the family, and the family is the backbone of the church and society. Healthy families begin with healthy wives and healthy husbands.

If I can help him become a better and more understanding husband, and if I can help her become a better and more understanding wife, then I have not only helped a couple, but I've helped a family for generations to come. I've impacted an entire community.

Let's be clear.

The last thing you need is a tool to help you pick out all the negative things about your husband. That happens automatically. I don't care how much in love you started out or even how much in love you are right now. The negatives have a way of introducing themselves to you in a way that you don't forget. Call it a "pet-peeve" or whatever you wish; there are things about your husband that get on your nerves. Once you admit it, you'll feel better.

What you really need is a tool to help you deal with the negatives, understand him better, grow with him, and strengthen your relationship. You can turn the negatives around to positives once you truly understand them. Wouldn't you like that?

This book and the companion version, "I Love My Wife, But" is just the tool you need to make that happen. It won't happen by reading alone. You must commit to making changes in the way you think and react. Take the questions and lessons you learn here seriously. If you treat this process as if it's the tool you need to create the best marriage ever, that's what it will be for you.

As I share what works for me and what I would do, remember this is a process of going from where you are to where you want to be. I'm here to help you take some key steps in that direction. If you take your time and seriously work on the questions asked, do the exercises, and communicate with your mate, this tool will transform your marriage. You will remove the but and gladly tell the world, "I Love My Husband, **Period.**"

This journey will help you. I promise. Once you receive help from this book and realize you need more – contact me at **rpthebig6.com** to schedule a workshop, seminar, or private coaching for you and your spouse.

Dr. Robert Pyles
Same Guy. Same Goals. Same God

Happily Ever After

"Every good relationship, especially marriage, is based on respect. If it's not based on respect, nothing that appears to be good will last very long."
-Amy Grant

For many of us, the decision to marry came after a series of interactions, conversations, and icebreakers, better known as dating. Believe it or not, it's on this battlefield that many of our wounded never heal, even though they go on to marriage. The reasons for this are many. One of them is a lack of respect. It sounds a little strange, but I'll explain.

Going into a dating situation is challenging when you consider the different combinations of personalities, backgrounds, and the baggage being carried. Just think of the different possibilities. When we are dating, we often have many expectations, dreams, and hopes that we wish to fulfill. Many of these dreams and hopes come from the movie screens, romance books, and ideas in our heads that are related to our past. Have you ever heard – no one marries a single person? Single, in this context, means an individual. When we enter the marital relationship, we are often a collection of experiences and prior relationships.

Many of us have the effects, hurts, and disappointments of past relationships carried as baggage in the new or present relationship. We never date a single person simply because we have all the other people and experiences in our history. Since they have not been laid to rest, they are alive and well to influence your present thoughts and dreams, even when it comes to a relationship or marriage.

Somewhere inside all of us is a small but powerful voice. This voice speaks up when it looks like our painful past is trying to get back into our future. Out of the past trauma and hurt, memories surface, pain is remembered, and that is when the voice speaks. It says, "I'm not going to let that happen to me again!" So, we make sure that we watch for the signs and throw out a test or two, always assessing and remaining insecure while wanting to be loved, but not sure if you can fully trust the lover. It is for this reason that many of us have decided to take care of number one. "After all, no one else is going to take care of me or fight for me; I have to." This is one of the biggest lies we believe. The truth is, in marriage, you take care of each other. You fight for each other, not with each other.

Many of us started dating with only one thing in mind, what would be pleasing to us. We didn't stop to think about the other person. We had an idea in mind, and we wanted it to be fulfilled. A request we hear often is to let him be tall, dark, and handsome. Or anything close to a movie star you've watched parade across your screen. Maybe you remember one of the best relationships you had in the past, and so you want him to be like your lost love. You created in your perception of his similarities and characteristics that look like what you once knew. Psychologically, mentally, or however you want to put it, you are loving an old lover while embracing your mate. That is scary.

You may not realize it, but you are living in the past. I know you would never say it out loud but, your hidden and secret desire is to love a ghost in your past rather than the dedicated person that stands before you. You see him through a lens colored with many faces and feelings from your past. Tell me, did you choose him because of who he was, or is he just a collection of all the good pieces of other lovers from your past?

Many times, we don't know what we want, we only want what we've known.

Even if you are fortunate enough to know what you want, it can be colored by images that we see around us. Going after an image and not after a genuine desire for that person is dangerous. To pick a Hollywood fairytale of romance versus the true essence of reality is not a solid foundation to build a marriage. We will discuss later that many have delusions about dating and relationships. It is the reason many wake up and wonder, "What was I thinking, how did I ever marry this person?"

Here's why decisions like this are dangerous; a person may have all these things they've ever wanted. Perhaps they have the Hollywood fairytale, but they also have extra baggage that you wouldn't want to carry. The things that make a lasting marriage have nothing to do with height, complexion, large bank accounts, the kind of car he drives, and so on. Just ask the woman who gets every little thing she wants but is living a lonely life of marriage. She is unfulfilled and lonely, sleeping with a stranger while being a stranger to the one she is intimate with - her husband. Those who have been around the block a few times have updated their list to reflect the truth. What is needed is a compassionate, considerate, trustworthy, loving, and kind soul to walk hand in hand with through life and until death.

You know love comes from the inside out, and so should the interest in dating and getting to know the other person. Selfishness begins to rule the relationship when one decides what the other should have or do for them, breeding a lack of respect because the other person's mind, heart, and soul are out of the picture. All that is seen is what you want and how to get it. Were you looking for someone loving, compassionate, considerate, God-fearing, and kind? Or was your first item on the list his height, shoe size, yearly income, and possessions?

Let's Go Deeper

If you want a better marriage, a better relationship before marriage, or are looking to help others in their journey of marriage, the best place to begin is where you will have the most impact – yourself. Think back over your past dating or marital history. How have things been? Think about the men you have dated in the past and even the overall outcome of the relationship or relationships. Do you see a pattern? As you look and try to find a pattern, stay away from generalizations like, "Yes, I see a pattern, all men lie, all men cheat, and all men can't be trusted." If you feel that way, I encourage you to find a counselor or therapist because those have roots tied to more profound issues you must address.

Take an honest look at your pattern. Do you have a habit of falling in love too quickly or not trusting as you should? Do you always seem to choose the wrong person or you find a good man but somehow end up losing him? Maybe even now, you are wondering about your present situation. If you are reading this and already married, it's a little late in the game to ask why you have chosen the mate that you have. If you feel you have been handed a lemon of a relationship, it is time to decide to make lemon-aid or lemon meringue pie.

Stop asking questions like, "What is wrong with him?" Begin to ask the deeper question. What is the deeper question? It might go something like this, "Rather than trying to make him see things my way, have I really tried to understand him? Am I assuming that I know all that I need to about him? Am I taking him for granted?"

Even if it appears that men are not responsive or complicated, they have characteristics that are just as emotional and sensitive as women; they just show it differently. Yes, men cry and feel. I have seen grown men weep like babies of lost love, a break-up, a divorce, or a cheating spouse. For some of you, that is a revelation; for others, it is not.

If you know that he has feelings, why not discover who he is emotionally, mentally, spiritually, and in addition to all the other ways that count. You will find that once you try to understand him and get to know him, he will respond and appreciate you like never before. Every man wants his true love to know and have his whole heart. Even more important than that, every man wants to be sought out by the woman that loves him. Just as you want someone to know what you like and need, he wants and needs the same. This requires commitment - a strong commitment.

There is a good chance that the "negative" you see is a reaction to your behavior.

Did you know?

"In the United States, researchers estimate that 40%–50% of all first marriages, and 60% of second marriages, will end in divorce. There are some well-known factors that put people at higher risk for divorce: marrying at a very early age, less education and income, living together before marriage, a premarital pregnancy, no religious affiliation, coming from a divorced family, and feelings of insecurity. The most common reasons people give for their divorce are lack of commitment, too much arguing, infidelity, marrying too young, unrealistic expectations, lack of equality in the relationship, lack of preparation for marriage, and abuse." [1]

I want to challenge you to deepen your commitment. You will find questions that will help you to uncover hidden truths about marriage and the one you have chosen as your life partner. Along the way, you will realize that you are not crazy, but rather that there are good reasons why you seem to butt heads, disagree, or even rub each other the wrong way. You will discover why you have those feelings of not being able to stand him sometimes, and why you love him more than anything other times. When you understand personality, it gives you a deeper understanding of why things are the way they are. You need to understand his personality and

---

[1] *http://www.divorce.usu.edu/files/uploads/lesson3.pdf viewed 11/2015 Overview p.41*

yours, and vice versa. When you understand this, it begins to chip away at the "but" until there is only "love." Remember, there is a companion series that addresses husbands and wives, so you can be sure that everything you'll read, he will too. If you want to know what I'm sharing with him, read the companion book once you're ***done*** exploring your role in loving him more.

I encourage husbands and wives to read the book together, talk about it, embrace it together. Complete the exercises without judgment of each other. Be honest and patient, after all, the rest of your life is a long time to live incomplete and unfulfilled – especially in your marriage. The strategies that help remove the but from our relationships are centered on mastering your personality. To learn more about this stay connected for my fall 2020 book release that will go even deeper into this topic.

Together we will unpack personality types that I describe as Earth, Air, Water, and Fire. Each type relates to the well-known D.I.S.C. personality assessments and the Jungian Type Personality Index of Choleric, Melancholy, Sanguine, and Phlegmatic. I'll describe my interpretation of the personality temperaments and encourage you to do ongoing learning about your personality and temperament through one of the mentioned philosophies.

I believe that professional counseling is not only meaningful but also necessary. So, as you are reading this book, if you identify that you need another level of care, I recommend you seek out a professional caregiver or therapist. This book is to empower you to love your spouse well and to empower them to love you well. This love is based on how you are wired and what you need. If each person in the marriage is focused on meeting the other person's needs, both needs are met, and the marriage is successful.

Chapter 1
From Dating to Distance

> "If God is going to write your love story, He's going to first need your pen."
> **-Eric Ludy**

Do you remember your "Dating" days? You made sure you were dressed fine, wanting to attract the right kind of man, you made sure your hair was done, nails set, and you picked out your clothes thinking "what if I see *him* today?" Sure, some days, you went for the natural look, but when you wanted to attract *him*, you knew just how to "turn it on!" When you wanted to, you knew how to turn heads. It didn't matter if it was working your greatest assets like your smile, your shape, or your stunning personality.

One day, you saw *him,* and just like you imagined, *"he"* saw you. You navigated through the rough and rocky waters of getting through the beginning stages. You asked all the right questions and found out whether he still lived with his mother, had or didn't have a job, and if he had a license to drive the car he was in (and, of course, making sure the car he was driving was his). After that, you checked for the obvious, "How does he treat women? Are we compatible? Can I see a future with him? Are those his real teeth?"

Finally, you check the details of your "research" and are pleased to find out he has a good job, a good head on his shoulders, and a pleasant smile with *real* teeth. Realizing there was potential, and that you've talked with him long enough not to be embarrassed to bring him around your family and girlfriends, you were happy to progress to the next step - seeing if he'd pick up the check at the dinner he invited you to. Having crossed all the bridges and moving through the hard spots, the two of you find love and look forward to the day you "tie the knot."

Remember when you thanked God for getting you through the bad relationships, the knuckleheads, and abusers? For a moment, reflect on the feeling you had when God brought the prince that won your heart. Remember that feeling and those memories matter, and when you hit difficult points in your marriage where the "but" comes in, it is memories such as this that can help ground you and remind you why you married him in the first place.

Your heart rested securely in his, and you were so glad to be in love together. Those were the good days. Remember? Think of those days of holding hands and hugging every chance you got. Dating had finally paid off, and you felt you hit the megabucks' men lottery! You scored, and he was perfect for you.

Do you remember talking to each other on the phone for hours at a time, thinking about each other, and smiling throughout the day and night? You thought the world of him, and no one else mattered more than him. You couldn't wait to talk, see, or spend time with him.

> *"The charming quirks become the things that drive you crazy."*

So how do we go from dating to *distance*? Years later, things aren't so romantic. The charming quirks become the things that drive you crazy. Let's face it; at this point, the honeymoon is over. And now that you've said I do, there are many things you wish he wouldn't do or say. There are habits you'd love for him to drop, and many others you may want him to start.

You are the perfect person to finish this book's title:

"I Love My Husband, But…"

I'd bet you could tell everyone you met, the story of how much you love him, and with the same breath run down a laundry list of things you would like to change. The funny thing is, he is more than likely saying and feeling the same about you. "I Love My Wife, But…"

What changed?

Absolutely nothing.

Everything you see now was already there before you said, "I DO!" You were so in love or looking through rose-colored glasses that you either ignored it or simply thought, "that's okay; I'll deal with it. It's not that bad."

The person that intimately knows herself is ready to get to know others intimately. I have found this to be true when it comes to dating; we know more about what we want than we know ourselves. We know our address, our high school, and we can recognize our immediate family members. But many have not taken the time to dig into the deep depths of their heart, mind, and soul. Many only deal with deep emotions when it comes to hurt, pain, and disappointment. It is only in those times that we stop everything we were doing and begin to think about the emotional turmoil going on within.

Usually, the only other time is when we are deep in love and are mesmerized by the feelings of love, romance, and dreams of the future. Just as it is with a lot of our family members, it is with us. We only get to see all of us at weddings and funerals.

The danger here is that in dating, we are attempting to find a mate. But many times, we do not realize who we are bringing to the table. We are only focused on who we want to come to the table and to be there for us. We may think that we're okay, or we may think that we are a good catch, but deep within, we are merely hoping that someone will find value in us and love us.

I'm sure you know what you like. But I must ask, do you really know who you are? How much time have you given to understanding yourself?

Let's Close the Gap

In a perfect world, you would have done the introspective work necessary to know yourself. In a perfect world, by the time you were 18, you would have been ready to be a full and complete woman when it comes to your emotions, your mind, and your values. The world isn't perfect, and not many had the training and parenting that raised us from this perspective.

If you are reading this, and your mate is reading the companion version, then you have every reason to smile. Even if you're separated, single, or dating, you also have every reason to smile. Why? Because this is your chance. This is your chance to get to know yourself on a deeper level and to assure that you are bringing a beautiful and precious package to the table. You are preparing yourself to move the *but* out of the way and love completely.

When we are finished, you will have a tool to not only better understand your husband, your sons, your nephews, but also be able to help them to be stronger, better, and more effective men. The added bonus is that this also goes for you. You will also be a better, more in tune, and empowered woman.

Chapter 2
Purpose Over Problems

> "Who we marry is one of the most important decisions in life. One that will influence the level of happiness, growth, and success, like no other choice."
> **-Nathan Workman**

Many times, in relationships and marriages, couples don't communicate as they would like or as sincerely and honestly as they need to. Sparing a few hurt feelings for the moment, they set the stage for hurting and disappointing each other later. Many times, putting off the hard conversation or the difficult issues only increases the hurt and destruction it will inevitably cause later. Just like "out" is always better than "in" – "now" is better than "later." You can't hold everything in, you need to get it out, and later can be too late, so you need to do it now.

When you delay addressing a problem, it can begin to distort your purpose. Living in pain, one mate may seek comfort elsewhere, in a hobby, a friend, a bottle, or another person's arms. As time moves on, and as the pain continues to grow, you realize that walking around each other as if on tissue paper is no way to complete your journey together. It doesn't work.

The problem is, you loved the early days of romance and new love, but now reality sets in, and you see things you don't like. Let's be real; you see things you can't stand and wonder what to do about them. You have tried sweeping it under the carpet. You realize that not saying anything about it only makes you more uncomfortable, angry, and sometimes depressed. In a state of mind like that, you may give up all hope. You may have even said, "I married the wrong man!" "I made a mistake; I wish I could rewind the hands of time." The truth is, there isn't a single, married couple that I have counseled that didn't have at least one regret or two.

> *"Look deeper, beyond pleasure and pain, to understand the purpose of your relationship."*

Some perhaps would make a different choice if they could go back and do it all over. But here is the good news, there is hope for your present and future marriage, even with this person whose faults are staring at you.

Look deeper, beyond pleasure and pain to understand the purpose of your relationship. I designed this book to be more than something you read but to be an experience you bring into your marriage. If you are newly married, contemplating divorce, or have been in your marriage for a while;

every couple needs tools to help them understand the person they married. Even if you have been divorced, this book may help you understand why the divorce happened by learning about yourself and learning about them. I want you to look deeper, beyond pleasure and pain to understand the purpose of your relationship. I'm sure you have become aware of what you like and don't like, want and don't want. Let's go further and think about what you really need.

What you need is not to waste years of your life by throwing away the marriage that you now have. You also need to understand the opportunity that is right before you. You have the opportunity to grow, and to understand the necessary changes that must take place in your life to have the marriage you've dreamed of. You were put here to grow, not to go happily through life without any problems. Realize, there are thousands of people who never get to experience the blessings you now have. Many women, just like you, wish they had a man to love, and a relationship that lasts more than two weeks. Embrace it; you are blessed. Some women would kill to be in your position, and yes, have the man that you have, even with all the things that drive you crazy about him.

I want you to seek to understand and not undermine the gift that God has given you in the man that you call your husband. I know that when he does things that you don't like, they rub you the wrong way. Let me remind you, that as he rubs you the wrong way, he is either polishing you or sharpening you. Do not throw away this divine opportunity to become better.

Maybe I Can Change Him

I have seen this in both men and women. The desire to shape and mold a person into the image you want is dangerous and disrespectful. You are not God and were not given the ability to shape and mold man for a reason. I understand the problem, and I've heard it all, "No one is perfect, and if I can just help him out in this area, etc." The problem is you must know when and where to draw the line. Helping a person to become better in an area they are trying to improve is totally different from manipulating, intimidating, or even lovingly insisting they change and conform to your desires. You are not his mother, so stop trying to raise him. He is not a pooch to be trained and rewarded with marital sex or sexual favors. It is a form of incest to be physically intimate with someone you are raising. Be his wife, not his mother. Love him as an equal, instead of secretly belittling him as a child. If he was wonderful enough to win your heart and marry, he is wonderful enough to keep. There is a hidden treasure in your man's personality, just as there is in yours.

Instead of changing him, I want to show you how to unlock his heart. I want to teach you how to unlock the blessings and promises that God has made to you regarding your marriage, family, and future. This being said, take this book and begin to understand the gift you have been given and the wonderful future that lays before you. But please be warned, as you continue to read, you will be challenged to grow and challenged to change the way you look at your husband – and yourself.

If you want to live out the rest of your years in happiness, growth, and divine purpose, then read further. If you are satisfied with being dissatisfied, and only living to complain about what you don't like, then read no further. I don't want to waste your time. I wrote this material so both you and your mate can read, study, and discuss each chapter together in the two different versions of the book written specifically to the wife and the husband. Take time to reflect and observe your responses as you consider the words and exercises within this experience. Even if your spouse decides not to read the book, read the book anyway.

I will use my years of counseling and ministering to help you and your mate discover the deepest depths of what God originally intended for your marriage. At the end of both books, there is a way to contact me. Relationships are within the Big 6 principles I teach to help individuals grow and develop exponentially. If you have not read my book Anchoring the Big 6, it is a good foundation for what you are about to experience, and I encourage you to grab a copy of it as well.

Are you ready to enjoy love in a way you never have? I'm prepared to teach you. We will start by exploring if there are problems you haven't addressed and reaching deep to discover how those problems are purposeful in removing the *but* out of the title of this book.

1) Do you feel you know all there is to know about your husband?
2) Are you secretly bored with your husband?
3) When was the last time your husband thrilled you or did something to make you think of him all day long?
4) After you have spent some time observing your husband, complete the following sentence – "I think my husband would experience more out of life if he would just…"
5) I would love to change the following things about my husband (list at least three, you know you have them).
6) When you think of your marriage, what is it that makes you happy and thankful; the kids, the house, the cars, standard of living? Name your top three.
7) Name five of your husband's favorite things.
8) When was the last time you made sure he had any of those five things consistently?

Hidden Problems in Plain Sight

If I were working with you through those questions, I could look at your answers and tell you where there are hidden problems in plain sight. There is always something more to learn about your husband, as the years pass each of you grow, and you never stop learning about your husband. If you are secretly bored with your husband, this indicates that you've not only stopped learning about him, but you are probably finding yourself completing question number four: "I think my husband would experience more out of life if he would just. . . "

Does your husband know what it takes to thrill you? He can't do something he doesn't know how to do or what it takes to do it, I'm wondering, even if it takes you stepping outside of your comfort zone, will you tell him what it takes to thrill you? Problems are magnified when either mate continually thinks of how to change the other one. The last thing I'll address in the questions posed above is, do you know his favorite things? If you knew them, that's great. If you didn't – start there. For those that knew them, how intentional are you in making sure he has them? Maybe it's not possible to give him all five all the time, but I'm sure there is a way to give him at least one. Finally, relax – remember there's a book for him too.

Chapter 3
Two Personalities One Marriage

> "To start the flow of oxygen, pull the mask towards you. Place it firmly over your nose and mouth, secure the elastic band behind your head, and breathe normally. Although the bag does not inflate, oxygen is flowing to the mask. If you are traveling with a child or someone who requires assistance, secure your mask first, and then assist the other person."
> **- Typical Airline Announcement**

Out of the millions of people that fly every year, it is not uncommon to hear the above quotation repeated over and over again. Even though you may have flown many times before, you will still hear this same statement repeated. For those of you that haven't flown, let me introduce you to the statement and the genius that it holds. I remember the first time I heard it and took note of the last few words. I was amazed that in this statement, the boards of directors, lawyers, supervisors, and upper management, have similarly all agreed that this statement was correct and necessary. Because it was never known ahead of time if specific pressures would increase to the point of danger, they devised a system that would make oxygen masks available, automatically. In this dangerous situation, they gave the instruction they thought was essential for the well-being of everyone. If you had a child or were sitting next to a person that needed assistance, you are to place the mask over your face first and then your child or person next to you.

What always amazed me about this statement was that the child of the person comes after the person's safety and care; this always seemed a little backward to me because I was taught to consider others first. In putting others first, it is not difficult to imagine that in a needy situation, you would take care of them before considering yourself. However true that may be, these are not the instructions that are given. The insight that I get from this statement is simple. You have to consider yourself first in some situations.

> *"It is best to be selfish when it comes to correcting or bettering yourself, and selfless when it comes to helping, praising, or complementing others."*
> *– Unknown*

When you think about it, it makes a lot of sense. In fact, thinking about it further, it is absolutely necessary. First, it makes sense because taking care of yourself first means that you are in a better position to help others. Without receiving the help you need first, it becomes more difficult, if not impossible, to help others. This means that you must be the focus and the attention of the help that's needed first, and then you will be able to see clearly how to help others. Without putting the attention on ourselves first, we run the risk of being self-righteous, and uncorrectable. If we do not focus on ourselves first, we will develop a habit of always pointing the finger at someone else. Does that sound familiar?

> *The way to defuse an argument is to point the finger at yourself.*

Arguments survive because each person continues to point the finger at the other person. The way to defuse an argument is to point the finger at yourself. Somehow, you will notice that the argument magically disappears. This not only works for arguments, but for misunderstandings, tough conversations, and any corrective measure that needs to be taken. I want you to focus on yourself before attempting to help your mate or significant other. This simply means that before you can begin to unravel the personality of your partner, you will need to dig into your own personality, habits, and mindset before attempting to understand and correct the same in your partner.

Let's make sure that you have the oxygen you need, before attempting to put the mask on your mate. This also means the only mask that is necessary is the one for oxygen. Therefore, I want you to take off all other masks that you can so you can truly see clearly. What did I just say? Be honest with yourself and breathe as we move forward.

Your Personality and the Elements

Let me ask you a question. How many times have you sat down and seriously thought about your personality? Or let me ask this question. When was the last time you pondered your psychological makeup or asked yourself the reasons why you thought, felt, or acted a certain way, and thoughtfully answered? If those two questions seem a little strange to you, then you probably are wondering just like everybody else. We often do not look at ourselves, but instead, we look at others, and yes- point the finger. Many of us are all too quick to look at and easily discover the faults of others while being completely blind to areas that need improvement in our lives. This is true for everyone but especially true for those who are in a relationship together.

Maybe it's because we spend more time with ourselves than anyone else, and we think that we know ourselves. The problem is, we do not know ourselves as deeply as we think. Many of us are strangers to ourselves. The one thing that we know is how we look when we get hungry and what we need on a fundamental level. But when it comes to who we really are, many of us do not have a clue even about our own selves. But that does not stop us from trying to correct others, or read other people's mail, or even tell them a thing or two. Even amid a heated conversation, we are so sure that we are right.

Without even thinking things through, we know that we're right, and we dare anyone to challenge us. When we are found to be incorrect, we feel ashamed or inadequate as if we could never be wrong. Every person that I have counseled, every person that I have helped, they were helped because they were open to correction, and open to understanding more about the situation than they did before. I want you to be able to understand more about you, your relationship, and the future of your marriage.

This is the wrong time to think that you have everything figured out and that you do not need any further information. The reality is your marriage and relationship is where it is because of the level of thinking and understanding that you have, and this is not a bad thing. I know it is not you alone, you're in this together. But you are a vital part of the equation, and as you know, any number divided by zero will bring everything to zero, you matter. If your relationship is in a great spot, then you can learn how to develop it further to be the marriage you've dreamed of having.

Your ability to think deeper and understand more than what you have before will be the key to unlocking new doors, and new avenues for your relationship to grow. Also, by being open-minded, you can learn more and achieve the goals that you desire in your marriage.

I am challenging you to open your mind and willingness to explore and understand your personality. I have heard it said that the way to get through a difficult subject is by making it easy to understand. Like telling a story, or a joke, we understand it and, therefore, can easily get the punchline. Sometimes making the point by trying to sound philosophical and scientific, doesn't get the job done. In fact, it can make things worse. This is why I have chosen to make the difficult and complex subject of your personality as easy and comfortable as possible to understand.

Breaking Down the Elements

The foundation of exploring the elements of your personality is knowing and understanding your pattern. Each of us has a pattern that we operate and react out of. It is as much a part of us as anything else. This pattern programs us as to how we react to stress or seek joy and affirmation. It also helps us understand what is and isn't important to us. One person's pattern may be that they are easily excited and talkative; another person may be sitting quietly and never saying a word unless literally on fire. You know the kind of person I'm talking about. You either know one or are one. There is also another pattern or two that covers the kind of person that is bold and outspoken. This person doesn't wait until he is on fire to speak; he sets others on fire. And then there is the person that takes things seriously and easily shows you every reason why the glass is half empty.

The way I describe our specific patterns is by looking at the elements. We have the four basic elements, and without them, we can't live: earth, air, fire, and water. In understanding your husband and removing the but I am sharing excerpts from my book Mastering Your Personality. This book goes even deeper into the highlights I am sharing with you now. Understanding personalities go back centuries, literally. A physician by the name of Claudius Galenus was a leader in developing the personality terms Melancholy, Sanguine, Choleric, and Phlegmatic. If you are familiar with the D.I.S.C. system developed by psychologist William Moulton Marston, you may know these terms as Dominance, Influence, Steadiness, and Conscientious. I am choosing to provide both references for the sake of guiding you through understanding yourself and your mate.

Earth (Melancholy, C)

What do you think about when you think about the Earth? What kind of personality type would the Earth have if it were to have one? Well, what we know about the Earth is that it's stable, hard to move, dependable, comfortable, and yes, predictable.

The Earth Personality is an introverted, logical, analytical, factual, private, lets-do-it-right person. Earth Personalities respond to others in a slow, cautious, and indirect manner. Earth Personalities are reserved and suspicious until sure of your intentions.

The Earth Personality probes for the "hidden meaning" behind your words. They are timid and may appear unsure and have a stern expression. They are self-sacrificing, gifted, and they tend to be a perfectionist. Earth Personalities are susceptible to what others think about their work. The Earth Personalities is well organized; on occasion, you may find an Earth Personality that keeps things cluttered; however, they know what's in the piles. The Earth Personality is determined to make the right and best decision. Earth Personalities will ask specific questions, and sometimes they will ask the same question again and again.

The Earth Personalities needs reassurance, feedback, and reasons why they should do something. They need information, time to think, and a plan. The Earth Personality fears taking a risk, making a wrong decision, and being viewed as incompetent. Earth Personalities tend to have a negative attitude toward something new until they have had time to think it over. Earth Personalities are skeptical about almost everything, but they are creative and capable people. Earth Personalities tend to get bored with something once they get it figured out.

Air (Sanguine, I)

Air is refreshing, light, and indispensable. What would an air personality be like? Air is everything mentioned and more, including unstable.

The Air Personality is an extroverted, fun-loving, activity-prone, impulsive, entertaining, persuasive, easily amused, and optimistic person. Air Personalities are receptive and open to others and build relationships quickly. They are animated, excited, and accepting of others. They will smile and talk easily and often. It is not unusual to feel as if you have known the Air Personality for years after only a few minutes.

Air Personalities are so people-oriented that they easily forget about time and are often late arriving at their destination. Air Personalities get bored easily because of their orientation to social involvement, activity, and general dislike for solitude.

The Air Personality never lacks friends and their attention span is based on whether or not they are interested in the person or event. The Air Personality can change their focus or interest in an instant. Air Personalities are competitive and tend to be disorganized. Unless very disciplined, the Air Personality will have difficulty controlling their emotions. They usually like sports of any kind because of the activity and involvement with other people. Their voice will show excitement and friendliness.

Air Personalities usually dress according to current fashion. The Air Personalities fears rejection or not making a favorable impression. They also fear others viewing them as unsuccessful. Air Personalities are very effective in working with people.

Fire (Choleric, D)

We have all encountered fire and Fire Personalities. Do you imagine what a Fire personality must be like?

The Fire Personality is an extroverted, hot-tempered, quick-thinking, active, practical, strong-willed, and easily annoyed person. Fire Personalities are self-confident, self-sufficient, and very independent-minded. They are decisive and opinionated and find it easy to make decisions for themselves as well as others.

Fire Personalities tend to leave little room for negotiating. The Fire Personality is a visionary and seems to never run out of ideas, plans, and goals, which are usually very practical. The Fire Personality does not require as much sleep as the other temperaments, so their activity seems endless.

Their activity almost always has a purpose because they are, by nature, result-oriented. They usually do not give in to the pressure of what others think unless they see that they cannot get the desired results. Fire Personalities can be crusaders against social injustice as they love to fight for a cause.

Fire Personalities are both direct and firm when responding to others. They are slow to build relationships because results tend to be more important than people. They do not easily empathize with the feelings of others or show compassion. Fire Personalities think big and seek positions of authority.

Water (Phlegmatic, S)

The Water Personality is an introverted, calm, unemotional, easygoing, never-get-upset person. Water Personalities are both slow and indirect when responding to others. They are also slow to warm-up but will be accommodating in the process. Water Personalities are by far the most relaxed person with which to get along. They live a quiet, routine life, free of the normal anxieties and stresses of the other temperaments. The Water Personality will avoid getting too involved with people and life in general.

Water Personalities seldom exert themselves with others or push their way along in their career; they just let it happen.

The Water personality communicates a warm, sincere interest in others, preferring to have just a few close friends. They will be very loyal to their friends and find it challenging to break long-standing relationships, often regardless of what the other person does. The Water Personality tends to resist change of any kind without reason, other than they just do not want the change to occur.

Water Personalities show emotion and are prone to be grudge holders. Water Personalities tend to avoid conflict and decision making of any kind. They are practical, concrete, and traditional thinkers. Their stoic expression often hides their true feelings. Water Personalities may be patient to the point of paralysis. Water Personalities are persistent and consistent at whatever they undertake.

Defining Your Element

I am sure that as you were reading, you were thinking, "Yes, that sounds like me, or No, it doesn't!" There is something about knowing the truth and recognizing a cold hard fact about yourself that is undeniable. You know when the nail has been hit on the head. You also know when you recognize a part of you, even in a description. I'm sure you have noticed a number of the attributes and character traits from the above descriptions. The question is, "Which are you willing to own?"

Some of the descriptions are spoken of boldly for effect. There is enough truth in the listed character traits to recognize yourself. Is it a perfect description? No, that is not the purpose. The purpose is not to nail your personality to the wall just yet. It's like the coach told his team-mate who was anxious to hit a home run. After seeing the player use up just about all of his energy with imaginary swings, he told him, "You have to get in the ballpark first before you can hit a home-run." I am merely trying to get you in the ballpark first.

Try This

Take out a sheet of paper or choose one in a notebook. Write down the four basic styles, "Earth, Air, Fire, and Water." Out of the general descriptions given, number, and name the traits that you see in yourself. Don't be surprised if you have a few of the others or a little of all of them.

Review your findings and notice the greatest number of items listed and the heading they are under. If there are more of one than the other, then we know where you "Ball-Park" is. What if you have an equal number in two headings like "Fire" or "Water." Don't be surprised.

Here is how you handle your fork in the road:

Sit back and relax. Think of how you are or how you would like to be *most of the time*. Here is where you will have to go with your gut feeling and allow your inner compass to guide and steer you correctly. How do you feel about being a (blank) or a (blank)? Ask yourself and allow your heart to settle on the right choice for you peacefully.

It's important to note there are secondary personality traits, as well as a primary type. For now, let's get you in the ballpark so that we can take you further into your journey of self- discovery.

I know what you are thinking, "I thought this was about my Husband or Significant Other?" It is, but remember, we must get you the help you need before you attempt to help him.

*Now that you have a hint of your Element and Personality Type, find and review the full description of your major personality type from the descriptions above.

Take this opportunity to get to know yourself a little better.

> *I have a fantastic husband. Here's the honeymoon part: I still think he's the funniest, wittiest, most clever man I've ever known.* - **Sarah Jessica Parker**

I have heard it and so have you, "You are just in the honeymoon stage, just wait." Maybe you have heard, "You two love each other, hope it lasts." Many well-wishers secretly desire your marriage to end up like theirs, miserable. I think misery does love company, but it doesn't have to be you keeping it company.

You love your husband for a good reason. Reading the personality types of Earth, Air, Fire, and Water, you not only saw yourself but your husband. I think you may have uncovered more about his personality before you had completely owned all of your own. I understand. I respect men and women alike, but I have to say that women are often more aware of their husband's feelings and personality. It has been said that women are smarter than men. I'm not going to touch that but, I will say that women can certainly be more perceptive if they choose to be. After looking at the personality types, you noticed some things, and you may have even smiled at how bits and pieces of your husband's personality were mentioned.

Let's look at the different personality types again, but this time, let's look at the positive and remember why you love your husband. No matter where you are in your marital relationship, it's always good to remind yourself of why you loved him in the first place.

If your husband is an Earth Personality:

You may love his thoroughness. You trust and feel secure in his ability to make decisions, and like that he takes his time. He isn't persuaded by the hype or excitement of others but does what he feels is right. You feel secure in knowing that his digging into the subject will make his leading and deciding the best way to go because he is reliable and secure. You also may feel his ability to "Keep it real" is refreshing, especially after dealing with deceivers in your past.

If your husband is an Air Personality:

You may love the life he brings to the everyday grind. He is the life of the party, takes care of his appearance, and is engaging. You may love his ability to be spontaneous and carefree. You may love the friendship ability to discuss things, especially in the morning hours or at night, when pillow-talk is a nice end to a long day.

If your husband is a Fire Personality:

One of the things you may love about him is his "Drive." You love the fact that he has plans and makes things happen. You wanted a man that had a vision, and you have one in your Fire Personality husband. You love that when he sets his mind to something, he gets it done. You have the confidence in him that someway, somehow, he will come through for you. You also love how he doesn't give up, even when things look bleak.

If your husband is a Water Personality:

It's easy to see why you would love so many of his qualities. You may love his easy flowing, easy-going way of dealing with things. It takes him a while to get upset or lose his temper. You may also admire his ability to feel and empathize with you. You feel that he is considerate and conscious of your feelings, wishes, and desires.

~

Take a moment to write down and review the many things you love about your husband.

I am asking you to write and review what you love about your husband. This list will be very valuable in times of storm when the sailing doesn't seem to be going as smoothly as you want. It is always a good time to remember the good in him.

You fell in love with your husband for all the reasons you've written down. As you write and review, you see the very reason you had a honeymoon season, to begin with; now that you have this, understand that you now hold the key to creating the honeymoon atmosphere whenever you wish.

Take notice. Even as you began reviewing, reminiscing, and smiling, your feelings changed. Notice that whatever you have been going through, you feel better about your relationship just because you remembered what you love about him.

Let me ask a good question that helps with the next section. When the honeymoon season ended, where did it go? What part of your husband are you experiencing during the bad times? Isn't he the same man you fell in love with?

Which would you say is true about you and your husband's relationship?

- We are two opposites that attract and find ourselves opposite on almost everything but stay together anyway.
- We are two opposites that attract and have found a harmony that helps us build each other up and provide what the other doesn't have.
- We are so compatible; it's crazy. We have more years under our belt than we've had arguments - We never fight.
- We are so much alike that we fight all the time. Most days I love him, other days, I wonder who's sleeping in my bed.
- Our relationship is complicated in that we understand what we don't like about the other person and are okay with it - it's our cross to bear.
- God has given us to each other, and I just want to be better for him.

- I want to give him what he needs.

Understanding Your Needs

Let's take a step back and take another look at you. Your personality type has needs. When you don't receive what your personality type needs, you feel less than happy. You don't like it and begin to feel frustrated as you continue to try to deal with everyday life.

When you are deprived of air, after two minutes, things become dangerous. You could die. When the body goes without water for five days, the same occurs. Death becomes possible. Even though your emotional, psychological, and spiritual endurance allows you more time, it's only a matter of time before you begin to die. Death on this level comes slowly and slightly at a time. It's an interesting thing but, even getting just a little bit of what you need helps but may do more bad than good.

Let me explain. Not getting what your personality needs makes you feel unappreciated, disconnected, and in survival mode. After a long while, you become used to not getting what you want. You become accustomed to living and loving in pain. Then, out of nowhere, you get a little crumb of what you need. Like a sip of water to the thirsty, you feel great and remember how good things could be. The danger is, going back into another long season of not getting what you want, you begin to lose hope. The thoughts begin to flood your mind that the little crumb you keep getting after so long a time, just isn't enough. As you continue to lose hope, you begin to fight the temptation to seek comfort elsewhere, like that nice guy at work who's just trying to be a friend. Rather than the little you receive showing you that there is hope, it becomes something else. Thoughts may enter your mind like, "See, he could give me what I need, but he just doesn't care enough to. I don't matter to him. He must not want me, or maybe he has someone on the side..."

You can't be the only one who knows what you need, and your mate can't be the only person who knows what they need. You must know and understand your needs and the needs of your mate.

If you are an Earth Personality

If you are an Earth Personality, you need patience and understanding. You don't need to be reminded of why you take longer than others to make up your mind. You need understanding and the freedom to go with what you think is best. As your husband begins to understand your need for information and the time to process things, you will feel free to do what you need to. You need patience and the time to process things and think things through as many times as you need to. It must be understood that you are simply trying to make the right decision and do the right thing.

You also need encouragement and affirmation. Because you may be tempted to see the glass as half-full, you need regular installments of affirmation, positivity, and patience. There are more needs, but these take you a long way down the road.

If you are an Air Personality

You need variety, engagement, and creativity. Your desire is to enjoy while being productive. You need to discover, create, and communicate. Like Air, you need room to flow, and someone to help you stay on task. As mentioned above, there is more to your needs, but these are your primary areas of concern.

If you are a Fire Personality

You need an inspiring atmosphere, a cause, or a challenge, and you need a helping hand. You have a lot on your plate because you keep it that way. Some may ask the question if you need stress to function. You simply need to feel the inspiration and vitality necessary to get and keep you moving. You need someone to be as aware and excited about your vision as you are. There's more to your needs, but with these being covered, the rest will follow.

If you are a Water Personality

You need an atmosphere of consistency, dependability, and stable leadership. You need a tactful and honest leader to communicate the direction you need to go while allowing you to voice your needs and feelings. You also need an atmosphere that is as stress-free as possible. Because you love and relate to others with honesty and integrity, you need others to have the same integrity and conviction that you do. Without it, it's difficult for you to trust.

Take A Moment

Now that you know your personality write down areas of need that you agree with from the descriptions above. Be sure to write down any needs that were not mentioned, as you will use them to share with your husband. Don't leave anything out. All of it is necessary. You may notice your list of "needs" is longer; there can be many reasons for that. One point of consideration is that you have a secondary personality, and that changes things a little.

Have you considered your husband's secondary personality? Do you think there are other needs not listed that he may have? What about considering if his needs have changed since you married? In the next section, I want you to look at how, why, and where you've seen changes.

1) Do you feel you receive most of the encouragement and affirmation you need from others or from your husband?

2) Imagine you are at home alone, and you can breathe deeply, relax, and be yourself. Are you able to easily feel the same way when you are around your husband?
3) When was the last time you felt like having fun or perhaps have been drawn in by an attractive stare? Was your husband included in this moment?
4) Are you still attracted to your husband?
5) How easy would it be for another man to steal you away from your husband?
    a. What would he have to say or do?
    b. How would he have to look?
    c. What did you feel while responding to this question?
    d. Have you considered your level of commitment to your marriage or relationship?

Chapter 4
Honesty Heals

> Positive feelings come from being honest about yourself and accepting your personality, and physical characteristics, warts and all; and, from belonging to a family that accepts you without question.
> **- Willard Scott**

When you think of the phrase "for better or worse," who wouldn't prefer the option of "better"? Better even sounds *better*, right? I think of a comedian who told a story about shopping for men in a shopping mall. I won't tell it exactly as he did, but I think you'll get my point.

There was a Mall where women could literally shop for a husband. Like many department stores, it had levels. As you can guess, the higher levels had better selections of men than the lower levels. A particular woman walked and was introduced to the men on the first level. Looking around, she easily noticed all the pot-bellied men who wore stained shirts, some with bigger holes than others. Personal hygiene was optional, but each of them smiled and welcomed the opportunity. The elevator arrived, and she went to the next level. There the men were clean-shaven, a little lighter on their feet, but none of them worked or had their own teeth. Dissatisfied and going through the next number of levels, this woman arrived at the last two floors. The men were fit and muscular; they were kind and cordial and even had their own teeth. The only thing standing taller than their average 6-foot 2-inch height was the stacks of hundreds they had. Each of them had pearly white teeth, honestly loved and respected the women in their lives, and earned over two-hundred thousand a year. She thought she died and went to heaven. But she thought and thought. "If this is the next to last level, what kind of men are on the next level?" She was informed the last level was a "Special" level that needed an attendant to accompany her. Finding an attendant, she got on the elevator and couldn't wait to see what she would find on this level. "Ding!" the elevator opened its doors, and she noticed the floor was full of women. Confused, she asked the attendant about the men on the floor and wondered why there were so many women. The attendant informed her, "This is the special floor designated for women who are never satisfied with a good man."

In this comical yet realistic experience of some women and men, instead of marrying for better or worse, they are in constant pursuit of better. However, better is a matter of perception. What is better for some is worse for others. When it comes to understanding personalities in relationships, "better" has a lot to do with what is wanted or expected. This goes even beyond personality.

Think about this. As a girl, you saw your mother and father's relationship and may have wanted a man like your father. If you didn't have a father, maybe you saw something on television or maybe even had a first love that was phenomenal. When it came time to marry, you could have chosen someone who was "like" all the positive relationships and experiences you had ever known. Add the unique needs and desires of your personality, and you have an interesting mix for what your "better" would be. I said it before, and I'll repeat it, "We don't always know what we want, but we always want what we have known."

We perceive better is happening when we are getting what we want. If you grew up as the little girl above, you might have seen your father as the ultimate model man. Expecting your husband to be another version of your father, you think things are good when you feel he's acting like your father. When you feel your husband isn't acting like your father, you may think he is not what you wanted. This also happens the other way around. You may choose someone to be the opposite of your father, but the same rules apply. When they don't act like your father, things are good, when they do, things are bad. Play the scenario out any way you want; whether you were looking for someone like a past love or even your father, your "better" could be just a comparison of what you have now with other lovers, or what you saw at home.

Is Better Good for You?

Tell the truth. If we had things our way, we would make things just like we wanted. We would be wealthy, could eat a cow and never gain weight, and certainly never grow old. The problem is, eating a cow, defying time, and being idle because of wealth, isn't good for you. The truth is, challenge, adversity, and hard situations are good for you. For many, when you get what you want all the time, it ruins you. Have you been ruined or spoiled by getting what you want? If you received everything you ever wanted, when you wanted it, you would become self-centered and begin to think that the purpose of everyone and everything was to get you what you want. The first person to feel this impact the most would be your husband. When something is spoiled, it usually makes others sick. Is your husband sick of you?

You know everyone, and everything is not here just to serve you. There's nothing wrong with breakfast in bed every now and then. As an example, think of receiving breakfast in bed every day. Breakfast in bed would no longer be special; it would just be the way things are. I said that to say, if your husband always gave you better, better wouldn't be special anymore. When we experience the "worse" it does two things – one, it makes us appreciate the "better" that much more, and two — it reminds us of the gift of our humanity, the way God designed it. You need a little of what "worse" brings to the table along with the "better." Let's look at a little of what you truly need.

Take A Moment

1) Name three things your husband didn't do for you that upset you.
2) Name three things you didn't do for your husband that upset him.
3) Were these things necessary like bills, picking up the kids, or something extra like fixing his plate for dinner?
4) On a sheet of paper, write out what would be "better" for you in your home and marital relationship. Don't miss anything and take your time. This isn't a race; it's a journey.
5) Look at what you've written for number four and cross out any items you already have.
6) With the items that are left, can you have a conversation with your mate about your "better"? Will he be surprised at what you need? Will he become angry?

Note: If you are afraid to discuss "better" with him, then it is likely you've had an occasional thought or two of leaving him or him leaving you. This means you need to discuss "better" with him sooner than later.

For Worse

Who wants to hear that worse is coming instead of better? I can't think of anyone that would rather have worse instead of better. Can you? I didn't think so. But, when you married, did you think there would be more good than bad, more better than worse. I know two people pitching in around the house makes things a lot better. Two people cleaning, cooking, and paying bills is far better than just one person having to do it all. Whether he cooks or cleans, it helps. So, you are right; some things definitely can be considered better.

Here's where you are so far, you know you can't have your way all the time and things may be good for a while, but bad or worse is coming. I don't want to depress you or tell you something that will hurt you. That is not my purpose. My purpose is to shed some light on your hard spots and the dark times in your marriage. You don't need help when things are going right. You need a hand when things get rough, and you feel like throwing in the towel.

So, how can I help you to see that even in the roughest places in your marriage, there is still good there? I can help you by pointing out a few things you should know. First, there's a part of the better and worse in marriage that comes from outside sources. These are things from places you didn't expect like, getting a pink slip because the company is downsizing after giving you a raise, one of the kids being sick or getting in an accident, and having an unexpected bill. I could go on and on, but you get my point. You and your husband must defeat those things that come from the outside to challenge you on the inside. Together, you and he handle whatever comes to your door, he may greet it first, but you handle it together. He needs you, and you need him to handle ALL the situations that challenge you.

This is a good habit to practice. When anything or anyone approaches you from the outside (outside your home), you greet it and meet it together. Whether its old friends, new co-workers, or even family, you greet it and meet it together, as one. This helps to handle some of the "Worst" things that could happen.

However, the most dangerous threats to your marriage never come from the outside; they come from the inside. This is where they begin, inside you and inside him, or inside your home. As I show you more and more of your personality with its weaknesses and strengths, you will see where you may bring a challenge to the marriage. For now, let's talk about him.

Both you and he have the power to destroy your own marriage. It doesn't take much. As I was told years ago, "It takes 5 million to build a bridge, but only $500 to blow it up!" Marriage and happiness can be very fragile and delicate.

The Pursuit of Happiness

You feel happy about your marriage when the top 3 to 5 things you value are being cared for like you want. If you value having a clean house, you are happy when he picks up after himself. If you like having a few dollars in your pocket, you love it when he helps you budget, plan, and contribute. If you like romance, you are happy when he brings flowers, kisses, and hugs for no reason at all. You have a list of things that you want to see, feel, hear, and experience because they are valuable to you. This is why they are called Values. This also means that they are not the only thing you want, but they are more important than the next fifty things you could name.

When you two got together, you fell in love partly because of what you saw, and mostly because of what you wanted to see. What was important to you was also important to him so, you got along famously as they say. You hit it off and decided to jump the broom and tie the knot. The only problem is, just as you have 3 to 5 things that are important to you, he does too. The other fifty things you could name are below the surface. Think of the iceberg that sunk the Titanic. To the naked eye, it didn't seem like much on the surface because what really sunk the ship was hidden underneath the surface.

Marriage is the same way. The things that challenge your marriage are hidden underneath the surface. Over time, and sometimes not long of a time, the massive pieces of the iceberg that were hidden underneath the surface shows. When it does show, the 3 to 5 things that are important to you are no longer at the top of his list. Things have changed.

The problem is not that he fooled you or tricked you. The challenge came because he grew and began to show some of his other personality traits. If you have an old- wineskin mentality, your marriage will not be able to stretch and grow as each of you grow. As time goes on, you will grow and want to experience new things, do different things than what you did before or in your early days of marriage. That is normal.

If you refuse to let him grow, you will lose him. If you fight his growth, he will grow to resent you. If you try to mold him into the image of your father or a past lover, you will be sadly disappointed when you realize that you have lost all three, your father, the past lover, and soon will lose him.

It is only your insecurity and fear that makes you want to control him by "helping" him to be "Better." Remember, your better is what you think you want and need, and not the real needs you have. You want and need love and security; you need affirmation and loving arms to encourage your growth and happiness. You don't really want to love and sleep with a version of your father, do you? You don't really want to sleep with someone you are mothering and scolding all the time, do you?

You may have loved seeing your mother being treated like a queen by your father and wanted the same. You may have looked for images of your father in every man you ever dated. You may have loved being cared for as daddy's little girl. I don't want to take that away from you, but you are your daddy's little girl, not your husband's. Don't make your husband your father, a past love, or anyone else. Let him be himself, and he will appreciate you for it.

Mistaken Identity

I am not saying you expected to marry your father. I'm being bold and saying some things that may shock or stir you on purpose. When you look at your father, you may see the character of a good man, and that is what you want. You may see in your father a faithful man, a bread-winner, and a strong leader; you may pray to end up as happy as your mom was. There is nothing wrong with that. I hope you see that too. The only thing is, you must never confuse the attributes for the man that was your father with the attributes of the man who was your mother's husband. Every man that I have counseled has all of the good traits of a man, but they may simply be misplaced or hidden by fear. (We will talk about this more, a little later.)

Let's see if you can answer a few questions that relate to how you view your husband's identity

Take A Moment

1) Does your husband remind you of anyone from your past? If yes, does he remind you of more than one person? Who are they?
2) Is your husband like your father at all? How?

3) Do you still hold fond memories in your heart of a past relationship, person, or experience? If yes, have you tried recreating them secretly with your husband? Be honest.
4) Answer truthfully, do you still "hold a torch" for someone in your past?
5) Do you live in regret, secretly wishing you had married someone else?

Secret Desires

Let's talk about question #5 above - "Do you live in regret, secretly wishing you had married someone else?" It can be a challenging question to consider, but it is a necessary question to ask. This is one of those questions that make you ask, "Did he really ask me that?" It is also one of those questions that make you scared to ask it, but also just as scared to hear what the answer might be. We both have heard, "Don't ask questions you don't want to know the answer to." I know it is a dangerous question, but when you see why I asked it, you will feel a little better.

Okay, let me say first say that the answer to the question is not my main goal. Breathe. Yes, I want you to answer the question truthfully but, the answer to the question is not the destination; it's only a part of the journey. I first need you to own up to the fact of whether or not you are living in regret wishing you had married another person. I want you to put a name, a label on that person only for the sake of identifying them, and the personality traits that you saw in them. I really should use the word perceive because you didn't really know that person as well as you may think. Remember the iceberg from the previous chapter? There was much more to that person than what you knew at the time. That person (if they exist) was valuable only because they held the key to what unlocked another part of your heart. You perceived that they were a certain way, and you admired certain parts of their personality.

That is good for several reasons. Reason number one is that the attributes of what you saw in them exist in your husband. He may show it differently, but it's there. Second, there is a part of your personality that valued what that other person from your past represented. What part of you wants this person to remain in your life? What part of you still thinks about them, is it your naughty, nutty, or needy girl? Have you shown that side of yourself to your husband, or have you been hiding her?

The last reason for going deeper into question number five is that it deals with growth. What is it about you that hasn't grown beyond that point of need or desire? In other words, why are you still there? In answering that question, you must look at what that interaction was doing for you. What were you getting out of it? A better way to ask is, how did this person make you feel? Once you answer how it made you feel, you can really see the person for what they really were, a key or a bridge.

This person was a key that unlocked other parts of your iceberg that were hiding under the surface. They were a bridge that took you from the normal, everyday living into feeling like you were really alive, or really in love, or really happy. That is the purpose they served, to simply help you see that part of yourself, and not to be the source of that life or love that they showed you. In reality, what they showed you was a hidden strength within your personality. It was only in your hidden desire to be and grow that you saw the need to hold on to them. Strangely, they were the key to you experiencing that part of yourself, the bridge that took you to a new place.

The truth is, you don't need them anymore. **You don't need them**. You don't need anyone else in your marriage, but you and your husband. It's time to give them the right boot of disfellowship. The way to get rid of them is to recognize what they helped you to see and be. Own it for yourself, and then release them from your heart and memory. It's as simple as that. You don't have room for anyone else in your happy home.

If this person were meant to be a permanent part of your life, they would still be with you instead of wherever they are. Release them and let them go; they have served their purpose. People indeed come into your life either for a "Reason," or a "Season." Stop getting stuck on the season and embrace the reason.

They were a simple tool to help you see and learn the strengths of your personality.

Take A Moment

1) Out of all the past relationships you've had, which one is the most memorable?
2) What made that relationship more memorable than the others? Was it pain, pleasure, or a combination of both?
3) List the things that are memorable and what you feel you got out of the relationship?
4) What would it take for your husband to get the same response out of you that relationship got out of you?
5) If your most memorable relationship was negative, how glad are you that your present relationship doesn't give you the same problem?
6) How and when do you plan to celebrate this and let your husband know you appreciate his love and care?

Chapter 5
Complex Issues With Simple Solutions

> "Always be yourself, express yourself, have faith in yourself, do not go out and look for a successful personality, and duplicate it."
> **- Bruce Lee**

I'm going to introduce a few subject matters that often cause complex issues in marriages. It's necessary to address these areas because if you don't, there will always be a but in your marriage, and our mission is to remove the but. Let's talk about finances, communication, stress, and sex. For the person tempted to put the book down (or throw it across the wall), and for the one asking, are you serious? Yes, and for a good reason.

You may think you have spent a lot of time with your husband and have an excellent handle on how they handle finances, communication, stress, and of course, sex. The problem is many couples that have been married for even ten years or more still have problems communicating their true desires. The reasons are many such as, "I don't want to hurt his feelings." Or, "If I say something now, he will know that I had a problem all this time," and so on. As time goes on, both marriage partners suffer and live unsatisfied. I've added this content to teach you how to understand your husband's personality deeper and see the potential in him. I want you to realize what he could be if you helped him make the changes he wants to make. For example, if you have a fire husband and you see that he isn't leading or taking charge, then you know he is feeling frustrated, and something is wrong, he needs you. I want you to compare his behavior with his potential and identify his need.

As we move through this section, I'll provide strategies for your relationship as it relates to finances, communication, stress, and sex. You will learn tips on how to bring out his best in every single area. Don't neglect to do a personal inventory as you are reading and compare how your personality also fits in each area. When considering yourself think of the support you may need to make the changes you want to make and how your husband can help you meet those needs. If you have not identified your personality type and your husband's personality type as discussed in Chapter 3 – Two Personalities, One Marriage – pause right here and go back and do this, it is necessary to move forward.

Take A Moment

Think of how you feel and what you need. Describe the kind of mate that would make you happy in the four areas we are discussing. This has nothing to do with your mate; this is simply the kind of wish list you'd write if the world were perfect. Don't go crazy, but please be honest, and realistic.

Finish the following thoughts:

1) Considering my finances, in a perfect world, my mate would...
2) Considering communication, in a perfect world, my mate would...
3) Considering stress, in a perfect world, my mate would...
4) Considering sex, in a perfect world, my mate would...

Consider Your Strengths

You have strengths. In times of high stress, comfort, crisis, or even a need to talk things out, you shine. That is why I want to take this time to highlight the strengths of your personality. Showing you the strengths you have will also help you to see the strengths your husband has. I also want to show you that the things you admired in past lovers also belong to your husband. In highlighting your strengths, I want to show you how the same power and strength can be found in each of the primary personality types.

Make sure that you know your primary personality type from Chapter 3. I recommend staying connected and getting my next book, *"Mastering Your Personality,"* Volume One, to learn even more about who you are and why you act the way you do. In *"Mastering Your Personality,"* I go through the personality types in great detail. In this book, I expound on the different strengths in personalities, and how they connect in covenant relationships, and conflict resolution.

As you read this chapter, keep in mind that we are discussing the romantic and marital side of personality types and their strengths. Remember; first you find yourself and work on yourself. Then find your husband and try to understand more about him—not change him. If he has areas he would like to change, then your role is to support his changes, not to initiate them or create them for him.

I will be laying out how each personality type views love with possible "Love Language" hints. Keep in mind; people are unique and different. No two molds are the same when it comes to people who have the same personality type. That being said, there are two things I would like you to keep in mind; understand there isn't a one size fits all for personalities and look for areas to grow and embrace them.

The fact is, you can't generalize or stereotype the four major personality types. Don't throw a big blanket over them and say, "All Fire-type personalities are all the same!" That would not be true. That's like saying all dresses are the same because they are dresses, or that all shoes are alike just because they're shoes regardless of whether they are pumps or flats. The reason is many factors must be considered. It's like having many cooks in the kitchen, remove or add one, and the menu changes. Another factor is the choices. The choices we make carry consequences that make us respond by making other choices. You understand this already. You have heard others say, "If you tell a lie, you will have to tell another one to cover that one." In this example, the first lie makes it necessary to tell others. If the choice to lie was different, the other choices to lie wouldn't exist. There would be no need for them.

As areas for growth are revealed to you, write them down and remember that your husband just like you are growing. This means he isn't finished yet. He isn't a finished product, and you aren't a finished product either. Sometimes we act as if we are complete and perfect in every way. The beauty of marriage is that two people come together to live and experience new things; out of it all, you grow closer, wiser, and more in love as time goes on.

You must invest time in reading, studying, and learning about personality, so that you will have enough resources to understand your husband. Pick and choose from the information you are about to read and piece together what you think is or is not like your husband. The same goes for you and your personality type. I can't say it enough; people are not "One size fit all," and neither are their personalities.

Consider that even though something doesn't seem like your husband (or yourself,) ask if it could be true. Leave room also for the unknown. It is possible that, just like you, your husband has many unspoken desires. Finally, think about some of the things your husband hasn't told you but only shrugged or grunted at in past conversations, or even joking around. Deeper truths could be staring you in the face.

As you let this information sink in a little, I hope that you will stop expecting perfection from him. (Don't worry, if your husband is reading the companion version of this book, I'm telling him the same thing about you!) You may not be, but it's always good to remind wives that their husbands are just as scared, insecure, and unsure about many things just like they are. Add to that feeling of having to play a "Macho" role, and you have the perfect setting for making many mistakes and imperfections.

Finances and Personality

Finances are critical to a family. Couples who argue over finances are said to have a higher risk of breaking up. It's not sex, family, or communication; it's finances. This is why you must understand how your husband's personality may deal with financial issues.

Earth Strengths
When it comes to finances, the Earth Personality can be just as dependable as the earth itself. When it comes to doing things, the Earth Personality says, "It has to be done right!" And yes, they have the definition of what right means. In finances, their perfectionist talents go to work.

Balancing a checkbook is practically a "must" for the Earth Type Personality simply because it is the right thing to do. Because they tend to be a little on the pessimistic and even distrusting side, they imagine that literally, anything could happen to the money. A bank teller could type a wrong number in and reduce the accounts balance, or someone could grab the receipt that wasn't properly disposed of and steal your identity and money. As an Earth Personality, they take pride in their precise calculations, often balancing the checkbook to the penny. Just as someone may enjoy putting a puzzle together or playing a video game, the Earth man or woman delights in comparing the checkbook to the bank statement.

Investing? The Earth Personality must do research, extensive research. In their eyes, not a penny is to be invested unless all the pertinent facts have been gathered, reviewed, evaluated, revisited, reworked, and rehashed. For the Earth Personality, each project is a NASA moon launch. A simple dinner outing wouldn't be complete without tallying up the bill. After all, the waitress or waiter could have made a mistake.

Want good credit? Let an Earth Personality handle your bills. This is not to say that every Earth Personality has good credit. I'm simply saying they can easily make it happen, more than many other types if they choose to. It is their meticulous attention to details that make them great accountants and CFO's.

Another strength is that they are not emotional or compulsive buyers. They can allow certain purchases if it falls within their budget and for a predetermined item or luxury. Even if they agree to purchase an item, it still must be the "right" item and at the "right" price.

Earth Weaknesses
You may say, "I Love My Husband But... when it comes to money, he's cheap, expects me to keep receipts, and balance the checkbook to the penny!"

When a situation calls for quick impulse buying or investing, you can expect resistance. They may even refuse entirely and let you deal with the consequences, washing their hands of the whole thing. Why? Simply because it wasn't done the right way. The Earth Personalities believe, on some level, that everyone should operate or at least understand that their way is the best way to handle such things, especially finances.

Even when trying to enjoy a purchase, the Earth Personality tends to bring up possible negatives or may say something to dampen the happy purchasing occasion.

Strategy

Let your Earth husband know that you appreciate his keen eye and frugal habits. Ask him why he thinks the purchase or financial move is the best. After he tells you, give him affirmation and praise, making his reason the reason for the fun and happy purchase or investment. Let him know that you are thankful and can rest easy knowing he's on the job.

~

Air Strengths

If you are in sales, you want an Air Personality to sell to. They easily see the benefits of purchasing, having, or spending on a particular item. With them, the check is on its way, and they will get to balancing the checkbook someday, maybe. Unlike the Earth Personality who reaches for the bank statement, they do just the opposite. "Okay, whatever, I don't have time to deal with that now, I'll just check the balance later." The Air Personality "Thinks" they have enough in the bank, and that's all that matters. Thinking more about how they will look in the new suit, jeans, or car far outweighs anything else. As far as the finances and payments go, "It'll be ok; it's going to be fine, I get paid in a couple of weeks." You have to love his optimism.

The Air Personality is open to financial suggestions if they don't have to follow it as a rule, and it helps their image. If it's fun and enjoyable, these personality types are open to new things and ideas. They see the advantage of spending, investing, and taking a chance. They are the right choice for supporting a purchase, an investment, or even a gamble. Just don't ask them where the checkbook is or about tracking their budget. Just tell him the money is in the account, and he may not mind you buying shoes and a purse to match.

<u>Air Weaknesses</u>

You could say, "I Love My Husband But… when it comes to finances, I have to do everything, or we are late paying the bills."

Your Air husband is disorganized when it comes to balancing a checkbook, keeping up with statements, and keeping a bill payment calendar. He often goes by what he feels when it comes to finances instead of the facts. Not only in finances, but he is disorganized when it comes to meticulous details and hates bits and pieces of papers and things that must be kept and organized.

Strategy

Your Air husband wants to do better and will even have a conversation with you about it. He may feel the responsibility to lead his family to better financial places than what he has done in the past. Left to his own, his credit rating may be challenged with a few bills in catch-up time. The necessary skills to balance the checkbook and pay bills on time must be put in terms he understands - luxury and leisure. Doing what is necessary should lead to a reward of purchasing a vacation or something that he has had his eye on. For him, the task must end in something enjoyable, fun, or satisfying.

Understand that his personality style is about freedom, fun, friends, and fixing himself up to enjoy any one of those. The pure Air Personality would not make the best accountant or CFO unless they have a strong secondary personality trait like Earth or Fire. This is not to say that your Air husband can't work things out. You would be surprised to know that just thinking of one's credit rating as social status or money not saved taking away from a lovely vacation can have a significant effect on an Air Personality. Remember, if put in the right context, the Air Personality can make the adjustments to get what it wants.

~

Fire Strengths

If you want something done as soon as possible, give it to a Fire Personality. No time to wait, no time to discuss it thoroughly, "Let's just do it already!" The Fire Personality is a "Take the bull by the horns!" kind of person that brings that same strength and decisiveness to finances. As task-oriented as his Earth cousin, the Fire Personality likes to get things done, only yesterday.

This is why the bank statement isn't gone over with a fine-toothed comb, but rather the bottom line or conclusion is all he wants. Your Fire husband has a gift. He can sum up an entire situation, conclude what should be done, and create a plan of action all in a single breath. He has no problem setting a financial goal and doing what it takes to get there. He feels that all he needs is your cooperation, and he can move the world. Financially, he has the strength to budget and stick to it, as long as he doesn't manufacture a reason not to.

He is a forward thinker and knows what bills he has due ahead of time. His mind is always going, and the family finances are a part of his focus. He has all the confidence in the world that he can control the finances. He will often attempt to strike out on a venture or tangent in hopes of increasing his financial standing. He always wants more even though the way to it may not always be easy or clear; he is still on his way to making it happen.

Fire Weaknesses

You may say, "I Love My Husband But.... when it comes to finances, he doesn't care how others feel, he just goes and does what he thinks is best without me!"

Fire can be bull-headed, not listening to anyone about anything, including finances. The Fire Personality must have a cause, a reason. This is both good and bad. Having a budget is good, but when the Fire Personality thinks of his "Cause" or many projects and ideas he has, he sees no problem with investing in them. After all, he is going to make it happen! He has no problem seeing the glass half full, and he's ready to pay for his share because he genuinely believes a full glass is coming. Yes, it's because he's going to make it happen! Did I say he was going to make it happen?

Strategy

The Fire Personality is goal-oriented and will dig their feet in and not budge to save the world. It often must be their way or the highway. This personality is task and goal-oriented. Like his Earth cousin, he wants results. Like his Air cousin also, he isn't concerned about the particulars because he is often making it up as he goes. This allows you to suggest a desired direction or change by asking, "Wouldn't it get you to your goal quicker if?" or "If we did this, we would really be able to change things!" Remember, the Fire Personality isn't married to the method to accomplish his idea; he's only married to the results.

Another note: Your Fire Husband is bent on "Better" and may never seem satisfied, always striving as if it's never enough. He must have a cause, and sometimes, he becomes that cause. Work with him and give him the inspirational air he needs to burn brightly.

~

Water Strengths

The Water Personality has to be the most supportive of the personality types. When it comes to finances, they show great strengths in being able to save patiently. That is true even though they may never get around to purchasing what they set out to buy. They may comfortably plunk a hundred dollars into a savings account every payday without any pain or discomfort whatsoever. This is simply amazing to the Air Personality, smart to the Earth Personality, and admirable to the Fire Personality. As Air thinks about what they could spend it on, and Earth things about how it's great to save for a rainy day, and Fire thinks about what they could do with it, Water just moves happily along, just thankful to be back home from the bank in time for dinner.

Budgeting and balancing the checkbook is something they would rather leave for someone else. They will try it and try to do an excellent job if it will help or make everything alright. When it comes to purchasing, they are comfortable if it isn't too much or too flashy, or something that will draw attention to them. Water Personalities are "go with the flow" kind of people, and they are of great support to the other personality types that show the intense drive in any given area.

Water Weaknesses

You may say, "I Love My Husband But...he doesn't have a preference, whatever I want to do with the money is usually okay. What is our goal?"

Going with the flow may not always be the best strategy. The Water Personality will often hold back their thoughts and go with yours. That means if another type firmly states they wish to go in a specific direction, they will usually say, "Okay." They may know what is best but usually will not say until pressed to say something. Finances between husbands and wives need to be discussed, and opinions stated. Here is where the Water Personality may suffer because they refuse to rock the boat.

Next to the Air Personality, they are the next profitable target for persuasive sales pitches. Flowing with different levels of emotion, they often use finances as a gauge of how much they will go along with your program or not. Often passive, the Water Personality prefers to vote behind the scenes. Because they are beings of consistency, they prefer to get on a path that works and stay with it regardless of your argument of how great it would be to change. In investing, they prefer a stable and sure thing, not given to chance or recklessness. If you need a spontaneous and right now kind of investor, this may not be the right person for you.

Strategy
Water wants everything to be all right and everyone to be happy. Like their Fire cousins, they can easily see the big picture when it comes to doing what is best for the wellbeing of others. They are huge supporters and will get behind you and do the work. To empower them to lead in the area of finances, they must be convinced that at the present time, it's the best choice for everyone involved if things are to be kept going smoothly. Water makes an excellent friend to Earth; water feels better when you communicate reasons for the need and how to get what is needed.

Take A Moment

Take out your Wish-List and match the characteristics of your wishes with the kind of person needed. Would a Fire, Air, Earth, or Water person be best?

Now look at your answer from the "Two Personalities One Marriage" chapter and see if you are the type that's needed for the job. If you are, any discomfort in this area is simply you wanting to sculpt your husband in your own image. Let him be himself. Perhaps you should take over the finances, discuss it. If you both fit, then make it a together moment as you work on finances.

~

Communication and Personality

Effective communication between you and your mate is key to meeting each other's needs. Problems in communication also rank high among reasons couples divorce. Communication helps you resolve conflicts by communicating fairly and listening intently to what your mate is saying.

Earth Strengths

Like Earth, the communication style is both thoughtful and deliberate. Not thoughtful as in, "Wow, how nice you were thinking of me..." but the other kind of thoughtful. The kind I refer to as the crammed with competing thoughts, kind of thoughtful. The Earth Personality has many thoughts, but they have even more questions than thoughts or conclusions. The Earth Personality is often unsure about themselves and would love to take the time to research and study themselves if only it weren't so psychologically intense and emotionally challenging. Their face rarely shows the depth of what they feel (as if they always know what they feel.) .

Their style of communication is very deliberate, and don't let their dry sense of humor bring you tears of laughter. Often not speaking very much, they say what must be said and then quickly stops as if to say, "I'm glad that's over." On the phone, they can seem quick and to the point while giving the impression that they really didn't want to speak to you when in reality, they did because they just spoke to you. Do not expect a bubbly response or a warm and sincere smile. Like their Fire cousins, the point is appreciated and should be gotten to quickly. Chances are you will never find an Earth Personality in idle chatter on the telephone for hours.

Earth Weaknesses
You may say, "I Love My Husband But... he doesn't communicate what he is feeling, and I only hear what's wrong, but never what's right or good!"

You can count on the Earth Personality to usually tell you plainly. Consider them a realist or even a pessimist who will share with you the reality of how things are. Unfortunately, it turns out to be the reality of his world, which is usually less than happy-go-lucky. He can be extremely literal, picking at words and meanings to the letter, and often reminding you of what you said in past conversations. While you are wondering if they were taking notes, you realize they are serious about being literal, which may shock you that they were, 100% serious.

Given to self-doubt and questioning, he asks himself questions like, "Am I going overboard, am I sharing too much?" Because his world is analytical, he thinks critically about everything possible, and he looks for consistency to prove what reality is. He may be easily confused by any mixed signals you give him because it is as if he is constantly taking notes to make the right moves in life. Lastly, because he communicates the "Real" side of life, you may feel like he always talks you down from an emotional high, a killjoy that steals your motivation or positivity.

Strategy
One of the best-kept secrets of the Earth Personality is that, like the earth that has lots of fire within it, so does the Earth Personality. They can be compassionate and emotional, even though it may never be fully communicated. Just as their face may never show emotional depth, their mouths my not speak it either. Just know that it's there. To deal with and persuade Earth, you need to be patient and simply communicate the reason for a given move or need, and/or the facts. Before receiving what you want from them, it's always best to give it first, constantly affirming and valuing them verbally, or with a subtle touch.

~

Air Strengths
If ever there was an area of strength for the Air Personality, communication is IT! The gift of gab is worked overtime with this one. They have absolutely no problem holding a conversation with anyone and

make some of the greatest storytellers. Whether the story is real or fabricated, he is sure to remain the life of the party for telling it. Air personalities are people. This is great for them because socially, they are rock stars. They love people and would love to have family and friends just drop by for no reason. Their motto is "Family, Friends, and Fun, the more, the merrier." The only thing more inviting than a spontaneous drop by of family is an outing, a party, or a holiday. Any special occasion will do.

It is for this reason that the Air husband makes friends and can kid around with perfect strangers so easily. He may never meet a stranger and seem bold and unafraid to speak in public or before large groups of people—many people like Air Personalities for all the reasons above.

This personality type can also be very quick on their feet and provide answers where non exist. As good storytellers, they can be very creative in communication. I have experienced Air Personalities making up whole stories and scenarios out of thin air. If in a debate, the Air Personality can battle like no other. If you need to be verbally defended, an Air Personality is just the type you need on your side. They make the best lawyers, actors, and politicians.

They are also good at negotiating and finding a happy medium for any two sides. They are born diplomats and can easily manipulate or deceive if they decide to use their gift for the wrong causes. Like Air dances and is free to go in either direction, the Air

Personality wants to be free to express itself just because it feels like doing so. Your husband wants to be free to communicate what he feels and thinks.

Air Weaknesses

You may say, "I Love My Husband But…he shares too much of our information with others doesn't know when to be quiet and is 'flirty' to other women!"

Because Air is a light-hearted and life-giving personality, it charms as it makes others laugh and feel comfortable. Other women may feel hungry for the excitement and attention your Air husband easily brings. It is a natural reaction to attach to whatever meets a need or gives you life. He is simply being his happy-go-lucky self. He is free with communication and may share too much at times. To him, talking comes as natural as breathing, and something to say as easy as the last thought in his head. Problems in communication can be oversharing, fabricating, or stretching the truth for the sake of dramatizing what they are talking about and being too personable or friendly.

Strategy

You deepen communication with your Air husband through storytelling because it is his means of communication. It is engaging and meaningful for him. Understand he has a need to communicate and needs your attention. Make him feel as if he is the only one in the room, give him plenty of eye contact, and ask questions related to the topic. Remember this; Air Personalities make some of the best actors. As you are interacting with him, just sit back and enjoy the show. Have fun; he wants you to.

~

Fire Strengths

When you consider the fire personality is concerned about the progress and getting things done, you will understand that your Fire husband isn't about a lot of needless chatter. I know your speaking to him isn't chatter. But, because his focus is on the task at hand, that's really all he truly wants to talk about. The fire personality is great at seeing and communicating the passion of a vision, idea, or goal. Since he is given to progress, he invites communication about what he is doing or how to get it done quickly because there are eight other projects waiting for his attention.

This is why the Fire Personality can be short on conversation unless it is meaningful. That usually means the things that he's working on or thinking about. In his mind, there is a ticking clock that is ticking down the seconds and minutes as you speak to him. It's not that he doesn't want to talk; he only wants to talk about the things that are crucial because his clock is ticking. He feels he doesn't have enough time to finish all the things he wants to. He prefers communication with brief and to-the-point statements because that is all that is needed.

Fire Weaknesses

You may say, "I Love My Husband But…he often says things that hurt my feelings, and he puts his projects before the family and me all the time."

The Fire Personality is the classic bull in the china shop. Your Fire husband has shown you the ability to take the lead and handle things. He rises to the challenge and refuses to back down from almost every challenge. His strength in times of adversity and in achieving goals is equal to his insensitivity and unwillingness to budge, even emotionally. To accomplish things, he may feel that there are emotional sacrifices that you must make, just as he has already made his sacrifices. Like tensing up in preparation for being hit, he has already made the adjustments to get the job done. He is only asking you to do what he's already done. He may feel as if it will all be worth it, and you'll even thank him afterward, but you just don't see it right now. He may feel that accomplishing great things calls for great sacrifices and effort.

Fire also burns. In passion for the vision, leading the family to better days and circumstances, even intimacy is powerfully felt by him. The Fire Personality also can passionately and easily win an argument. You wouldn't want to challenge a Fire Personality half-heartedly. Remember, Fire burns. There may be times when you feel as if you can't get through to this bull-headed Fire Personality. Trust me; he's considering what you said even if he doesn't show it or act on it.

Strategy

Get with his vision, quest, goal, or whatever he's trying to do. With the Fire Personality, remember it's easier to steer a fire truck from inside it than outside it. Your challenge is to see where his vision will take the family and deal with reality from his perspective and timetable. From there, you can ask, suggest, even question in a way that gets more results than fighting.

When he senses a battle, he takes it as a threat to his authority and ability to lead, and he will work to gain more control. While being able to get results and take control without controlling everything and everyone, a threat is perceived as a battle call.

~

Water Strengths

This reserved personality type is best described with a communication style that resembles still waters that run deep. Thinking and feeling more than they express, they would rather quietly show you than to yell, scream, or act out. This type thinks before speaking and appreciates words spoken in sincerity and truth. With this kind of communicator, trust is everything. If they feel they cannot trust you with what they are saying, they will not flow well with you.

When Water Personalities speak, know that they are speaking from the heart and are just as honest and sincere as they want you to be. They often do unto others as they want done to them, especially in communication. Just like their pace and sense of urgency, their communication style is usually calm and inoffensive. If you want kind and cordial conversation, then this Water Personality has just the flow for you. There is so much about them that says, "Peace," if not, "Leave me alone, I don't want to be bothered with that right now."

Patient in communication, it may take some time for them to get back to you, respond with an email, or even text. One of the things you love about your husband is that he goes with the flow and is slow to anger. Remember, there are two sides to this coin.

Water Weaknesses

You may say, "I Love My Husband But… he doesn't have enough ambition or motivation. It's like he has no goals and settles for anything - he's too easy-going."

In order to lead, this type needs lots of information about what's expected and a detailed outline of the authority; they have to get things done. They can lead when they're fully equipped. Their motivation is found in the flow that comes from consensus. Because the world seems to be an uncertain place to them, their act of preservation is to find safety in numbers and act accordingly. This means that Water often needs others or even an outside force to help them move.

Strategy

Communicating with Water is to be done peacefully and without confrontation. The best way to destroy Water's motivation and will is to become confrontational and belligerent. Don't do it! Trying to move the Atlantic is easier than to persuade a Water Personality back into your camp after you have offended them time after time. If you want your Water husband to lead, then assure him you are behind him with sincere appreciation, patience, and encouragement. Like trying to carry a large kettle of water without spilling it, you must be careful, patient, and move very easily. Still waters run deep, but when they start to run, it's hard to stop them. Sit down and have a heart to heart with your hubby and empower him to lead with sincere appreciation and respect. Ask him about his desires and goals and ask how you could help him to do and be more. Don't be afraid to show all your heart with him, he appreciates it and finds comfort in your honesty.

Take A Moment

Take out your Wish-List and match the characteristics of your wishes with the kind of person needed. Would a Fire, Air, Earth, or Water person be best?

Ask your husband to share his element with you if he hasn't done so already. No matter what element he is, you can help him by keeping his communication personality in mind while you are talking with him.

Stress and Personality

Okay, what doesn't kill you makes you stronger right? That's actually not true, and there are proven studies that suggest stress can kill you. If stress can kill a person, it can, without a doubt, kill a marriage. You have to know how to manage stress according to your personality and your husband's personality.

Earth Strengths

Some personality types deal better with stress than others. One type has found a way of deflecting their ball of stress. Another type meets it head-on and refuses to back down. Another retreats from stress and even may avoid it like the ostrich hiding its head in the sand. And then there's the final type that can become so agitated with stress that they may burn themselves out thinking up a solution to deal with it. For this leader of the household, stress and the demands of having to make quick decisions present new threats to the marriage.

Stress alone builds up like an emotional time-bomb that causes the Earth Personality to be agitated, angry, or to panic. When these individuals begin to think that they opened the door to this problem by not foreseeing what was ahead of them and preparing for it, it makes things a little worse.

Here is where the practice of not showing all of their emotional cards comes in handy. This type can keep calm enough to think about things and make decisions before completely breaking down. In stress, this personality type is busy thinking from all the different angles. They want to know where this threat came from, how it is that they did not see it before, the time frame that is in front of them, and what is the best way to defuse the situation while trying to solve the problem. The good news is, they have the ability to get this done. Earth Personalities make great poker players. Once again, their face doesn't show the turmoil within.

Earth Weaknesses

You may say, "I Love My Husband But... when things go bad, he thinks the worst and almost goes into depression when I need him most!"

Your husband takes things personally and internalizes not only this failure but every failure he's experienced. That is just what he may perceive it as – a failure to correct the problem through organization before it happened. To cope, you find him spending more time alone and licking his wounds in quietness. He mentally and emotionally punishes himself, thinking he should have known better or known that this would or could happen. Because perfection is his goal, he often kicks himself for not being able to live up to the standards he blames the world for not having. Seeking to control what he cannot only frustrates him further. After realizing the world isn't such a bad place and attempting to look at things on the bright side, he momentarily snaps out of it until the present situation reminds him again. Control can and often does become an issue; it's how he deals with the uncertainty of the world. This may only cause him to sink deeper into his own little world with its self-imposed emergencies and unattainable standards.

Perhaps the greatest weakness of the Earth Personality is the loudspeaker in his head that makes sure he hears all the negative self-talk he keeps rehearsing. He, more than any other type, will speak to himself negatively or negatively refer to his world – 75 times out of a hundred. For him, compliments are rare if existent at all. But don't worry, he doesn't only treat you that way, he does the same to himself.

Strategy

In stress, the Earth Personality needs to be reminded of the good they have done and the wonderful things they have accomplished. They must be reminded that the present situation is just a challenge like all the others they have overcome. Since they view the glass as half-full, and that there's a hairline crack that is causing more water to leak out, you have to maintain an atmosphere of positivity. Just don't pour it on too thick, he won't believe it if it is. Lastly, help him to break down the problem logically or even analytically.

Suggest tackling the problem or challenge by using baby steps. Encourage him; he can do it.Suggest tackling the problem or challenge by using baby steps. Encourage him; he can do it.

~

Air Strengths

"It will be all-right. I'm not worried about it!" might be the response of your Air husband. He may often deflect any given problem even if he is the reason it exists. It may be that he simply does not want to feel bad or feel the pain of the problem. Don't be fooled; he is not ignoring the problem. This is just his way of dealing with the problem. While the Water Personality may respond to stress by sidestepping and ignoring it altogether, the Air Personality not only does the same but seeks to have a little party to make up for the inconvenience. Air's strength is in the bright side and the cloud with the silver lining they own. Another resilient personality type, the Air Personality refuses to take doom and gloom for a final answer. Their ability to smile in the midst of the storm is given them by their other ability, the strength to overlook the minor details. Yes, Air types do get upset, cry, and even low emotionally like any other type, but will soon be over it in the next two minutes. Why? Because there simply is no time for tears, tears aren't fun and exciting.

This type knows how to turn the tables on stress and problems. They know how to handle it well because they bring both stress and problems from their procrastination, ignoring important information, and shopping. They know how to loudly hum along in their heads and drown out depression and stress with their favorite song. If they don't have a song, they will call a friend and cheer up by going out, or for a bite to eat. Men love to eat, and your husband doesn't mind hanging out with the fellas.

Air Weaknesses

You may say, "I Love My Husband But...he doesn't take problems seriously and doesn't take care of business like he should!"

If there was ever a personality type that was more faith-full, it's this one. They have a way of just knowing that everything is going to be alright. Sometimes, their faith doesn't have a leg to stand on. And in other times, they remain so optimistic even after they created the problem to begin with. The, "It's going to be okay" attitude of the Air Personality makes those around him wonder if he's dealing in reality or not. Truth is, he is dealing in reality. He places a great deal of faith in being able to talk his way out of almost anything, including talking to himself to do the right thing. Yes, he listens to himself.

You would like him to handle business a little more efficiently and not wait until the bill collector's call. You also want him to think ahead more often and arrange things a little better.

Strategy

You may be able to learn something from your husband in the way he deals with stress. Notice that he rarely lets anything get him down. Despite the fact that he gets himself into many of the jams he gets himself into, he knows how to handle it. It helps to communicate with him how much better it is to keep things alive and fun by taking caring issues before they happen. He will think you are trying to pull him down if you continue to point out how he is responsible, or the cause of the problem. Don't spend time trying to convict him or shame him. This drives him away from you instead of toward you.

~

Fire Strengths

Oh boy! Here is one for the books. Fire's reaction to stress may be described as fuel for the fire. The Fire Personality seems actually to need a certain level of stress. Want to see a personality type shine brighter than ever? Put the Fire Personality in a little stress, and you usually get a noble warrior that will fight for his cause. All of his admirable qualities seem to rise to the occasion. Refusing to take no for an answer, this personality type just knows there is a way out. Often declaring so in the heat of the battle, he can easily come up with a plan or an idea right on the spot. In the heat of battle, he is most creative thinking on his feet and moving full speed ahead, creating the road ahead of him as he goes.

This adds to his level of stress and sends him into overdrive. Whatever you do, don't get in his way at this point. He's a loaded locomotive that is running full speed ahead. Speaking of speed, he needs a certain pace. Things have to flow at a certain speed for him – fast is usually best. This is why he often walks as if he's going to put out a fire.

For this reason, you may also say, "I Love My Husband But. . . he is so impatient and is always wanting to rush me. I'm never quick enough for him!" This is just his pace for getting things done and is a means for him to be inspired. When he's asking you to move quicker or, "Hurry up!" he is only asking that you help him provide the environment he needs for motivation. He simply wants to know you are with him. Your speed demonstrates that you are with him in getting results quickly. This is the world he lives in, and he's glad you are in it.

Fire Weaknesses

You may say, "I Love My Husband But...he is too driven. He creates three more projects before the last one is done. It's like he's always thinking of what's next and never rests."

Somewhere within his programming, his optimism and high hopes cause him to dismiss a few of the necessary steps and rules he needs for success. It is as if some of the rules don't apply to him. It is as if he decides what he will do and thinks, "I'm going to make this work." When he finds out that brute force and running over things like a bulldozer don't work, he sits in frustration and then considers finding the information he needs to make things work. Because he is gifted, talented, and intuitive, he often does great things without even trying. Because he knows he can make many things work the way he wants, he often wastes a lot of time fighting a problem rather than solving it. Fire has to live leaning into the wind so that its inspiration and fuel to burn is fresh and constant.

Strategy

The Fire Personality isn't stressed out by stress but fueled by it. What frustrates the Fire Personality is simply a lack of results and wasted time. This personality type MUST see progress being made in his area of focus. All your Fire husband needs are resourcefulness and a dream or a cause. If you think he is stressing himself out, know that it is because he isn't getting the results he would like. Point his attention to the resources he has or even talk about his vision or dream. He will greatly appreciate you co-signing his dream or cause and admire you for it. The best strategy for dealing with this type of personality is to remind them of their dream, point them to their resources, and then get out of their way.

~

Water Strengths

I used to think that the old saying, "A watched pot never boils," wasn't true. The saying simply means that if you are in a hurry to boil water, it will seem like it's taking forever as you watch and wait. Putting the Water Personality in stress is like trying to boil a swimming pool of water in a hurry. Like his Earth cousin, when the Water is finally moved to an emotional place, it can be very difficult to get them to move away from the offense. They remember when.

Still waters do run deep, deep with reasons to either stick by you or abandon you, but you may never know the full reason why. They are non-confrontational and are more than likely to side-step stress altogether. The Water type flows best with easy-going settings where the love and endearment of family and friends are felt deeply. Even in moments of stress, their loyalties remain true as long as they are convinced it's the right thing to do and the right way to be. Water Personalities make the best friends and may never let you know they are angry with you unless pushed over the edge.

Water Weaknesses

You may say, "I Love My Husband But...nothing I say or do moves him. It's too hard to get him going, and he only stays motivated for a short time!"

The Water Personality takes this philosophy seriously. They feel no need to conform to any given mold or form that takes them outside their comfort zone. With them, it's all about emotional, psychological, and physical comfort. To accomplish this, they have a handle on what consistently works and develop a routine around it. They are assured their consistent efforts will patiently win in the end. This means not getting upset at every little wind that blows. Including a wind of excitement that you happen to feel at the moment or an item of importance you feel they should get excited about. For them, whatever is real can stand the test of time, and so that is how everything is tested. Akin to their Earth cousins, consistency and time-proven methods reign supreme. Without the research of the Earth Personality, they just intuitively know and feel what the right thing is. They go with their gut feeling regardless of you being on fire or not.

Strategy
Don't expect an emergency on your part to be an emergency to a Water Personality. Mellow and easy-going, it is almost as if they don't care about too much about anything, but they do. Find out what your Water husband's "flow" is. In other words, find out what his normal and comfortable style and pace is. He can be motivated by a goal if it can be accomplished within his flow. He is motivated but shows it with slow, consistent, and lasting habits. He will support you and help without demanding to be seen and heard. Allow this strong and silent type to help you and lead in a manner that is comfortable for

him. Remember, once his waters are stirred, he won't forget the turmoil you caused or the agitation you keep stirring up. You must calmly and gently surf these waters.

Take A Moment

Take a look at the kind of person you need from your wish list and compare what you have with what's on your list. With stress, you may have to help out a little. Here is where you come to the rescue. Looking at your husband's element, ask yourself what he needs and wants, then ask yourself what you can do to make that happen for him. In stress, he needs you. He can work on change later; in stress, he needs comfort.

~

Sex and Personality

Sex is a part of marriage, and each element has its own sexual personality. If partners understood this, it could lead to greater fulfillment in the area of intimacy. Needs are best met when they are understood; many sexual issues in marriage are simply a lack of understanding personality traits as they relate to the sexual needs of the other person. We will not only look at each personality strength but also their sexual and intimate characteristics.

Earth Strengths

When it comes to intimacy, Earth wants to pencil it in. It's not that your Earth husband doesn't want emotional intimacy or marital intimacy; it's just that he doesn't want to go into it without some sort of planning and foresight. Earth has the ability to plan, but it becomes a little bit of a hindrance when it comes to intimacy. The problem is, you can't plan true intimacy or calculate when will be the best time for being intimate. Even in times when he is open to a little spontaneity, he is usually thinking about his role and whether his performance will be acceptable or not. To the truly comfortable Earth husband, he uses intimacy to reveal the secret person he's been hiding and the passionate man he rarely let's out to play.

Earth can soar when it comes to both physical and emotional intimacy if allowed to fully grasp what is required, expected, and desired. He likes to set the mood in preparation, and so he will really plan it out with candles, music, flowers, and lots of romance. He can comply with your wishes and will be glad to do so, knowing it is emotionally fulfilling your needs. Not much for words, you can rest assured that whatever he says, it has taken some effort, honesty, and desire. To the Earth Personality, speaking intimately can be as serious a deal as spending money on a shopping spree.

Earth hopes you understand what he doesn't say as much as what he does. There is always a thought in his mind, and in intimacy, the selfless Earth husband is putting together the facts about you. He takes note of what you say you want and like. He thinks about you and is glad that he has an anchor like you in his life. He thinks of ways to please you even though he may not tell you what he's thinking. For him, intimacy and dealing with you can be the mix between a game and a science project. He is taking you seriously, but this is just the way he thinks of things. It's not a game because he is very serious about you even though some of the things you say may make him question.

In Intimacy

Earth communicates intimacy as he pulls from his storage. It isn't the moment that he's focusing on but what he has been wanting to communicate for a while. He understands the world and life but hasn't completely figured you out yet. This means that on some level, he is uncertain or even confused about something you said, did, or even a particular trait of yours. You can rest assured that there is something about your personality or habits that he would like to tweak. What you will get out of him is mostly what he is sure of. He is sure because he has been thinking about it for a long time and has taken notes on what not to do or say. He has been studying you. Because he has standards and expectations, he is pleased with a good chunk of who you are and won't mind sharing with you. He won't tell you or share his whole heart with you all at once, no matter how much he trusts you. He feels as if you knowing his whole heart puts him in a vulnerable state. Secrecy is power to him, for some strange reason. In intimacy, he trusts the person that will genuinely care about him. He trusts the person that is honest and consistent in their habits and communications. This is the person that wins the key to his secrets.

Sex

In marital intimacy, the experience is much like the Earth Personality. On the outside, he seems to be cautious if not rigid and uninviting. However, the core of the person you engage with is quite the opposite. The Earth Personality has a great deal of passion and desire that may need just the intimate escape it is getting in intimacy with you. Earth is not really a hard nut to crack but is just as true to the analogy. The outside may seem difficult to break through, but the inside is much softer and inviting.

Breaking through the shell and engaging the intimate Earth Personality, Earth let's go to enjoy the experience without judgment or apprehension. You will see that some of Earth's most enjoyable moments are found in his natural expressions and moments when his responses have not been calculated. Earth usually thinks himself in and out of trouble. However, in moments of deep intimacy and transparency, he flows freely from the heart.

After a while, when it's over and it is business as usual, he may be a little ashamed or even feel vulnerable that he let his deepest heart and feelings out in the open. Part of him is reserved for the "What if" of future betrayal and rejection.

Strategy
If you can weather the occasional pessimism, doubt, or cynicism, you gain the best of both worlds in your Earth husband. Like his Fire cousin, you have to work with him from the inside out. The Earth husband is analytical, calculating, and often reads between the lines. Your strategy should always be one of honesty and transparency, even though he may be a little scared at first to be the same way with you. He is making up his mind if he should share his secret self with you fully while taking notes to see if you are consistent and trustworthy. He may have married you but will operate with you on a safe and calculated basis. To him, "You never know what someone might do…" Winning his heart and trust is an achievement. Be proud of yourself for doing so.

~

Air Strengths
Your Air husband can certainly be the life of the party. Whether it's a room full of family and friends, or a private party for two, Air is the way to go. The Air Personality may be a little bit too much for Earth, and possibly even Water at times. Air overwhelms Earth with transparency and an abundance of emotional content that will only be liked and accepted

by the Earth Personality that has a secondary fit like Air, Fire, or Water.

Air has a way of hitting the heart in intimacy when the focus is taken off of them, as they begin to focus on you. The Air Personality has to pull away from the fun of the moment and begin to experience the other person selflessly. Since Air loves to be the center of attention, they love receiving attention. This translates to a love of affection when it comes to intimacy. The Air Personality has to become more aware of what the other person is feeling and wishes to say. Air makes the mistake of thinking that the moment is about them, and sharing becomes a chance to talk about themselves. Like opening Pandora's Box and never being able to return, the Air Personality can begin sharing and hardly ever stop. It is their love of communication and sharing that opens the floodgates and will sweep the entire moment away if allowed.

In Intimacy

Air lives to ride the wave of the moment. Throwing care to the wind, the Air Personality may willingly open their heart and mouth just to see what develops. They are intuitive and may be able to lead the conversation or may feel they need to pull out something that might be fun to explore. With your Air husband, intimacy may be more like a game than a painful display of emotions. The Air Personality loves being open and free with sharing. Like the wind itself, the Air Personality is unpredictable when it comes to what they may be thinking and feeling. A true emotional roller-coaster ride, the Air Personality delights in the twists and turns of their emotions and thoughts. Sharing their feelings can give the Air Personality a "high." The only thing that is more enjoyable to the Air Personality is receiving what they give to others. Air feeds on Air and can build to a kind of mental and spiritual tornado that erupts in one enjoyable experience after another. The danger is, Air has to be grounded sooner or later or it may just drift off into the depths of space and never return.

Air will share what is thought and felt with a stranger, which is why they never meet a stranger. At times, it seems like Air is a little too free with itself. This makes the companion of Air question loyalty and faithfulness when Air is simply being its simple yet transparent self. Since other personality types are not as free to share their heart and feelings, the Air Personality seems bold and powerful. Just as the air we breathe is delicate and light, so is the fragile heart of the Air Personality whose sole desire is to be liked, accepted, and celebrated.

Sex

The Air Personality can be very expressive when it comes to marital intimacy. Air wants physical intimacy that is spontaneous, different, and fun. They love a creative twist instead of the same-old, same-old. But don't worry, in verbal intimacy, they will freely share what they want. If you give them a chance, they will even come up with ideas and changes in the bedroom for you to say yes to. Just ask Air the simple question, "What do you want to do. . . ?" and they will let you know. Don't be surprised if they suggest an idea or a place that you never thought of. The freedom that they share in enjoying life gives them the power and practice needed to express themselves fully. Air is not always focused on itself. Remember, Air wants to be noticed, accepted, and admired. This means that Air will try to please in order to receive the needed level of acceptance. Your Air husband wants to be all that you will ever need, and loves to hear your truthful and honest praise and acceptance. Air is open to the physically intimate moment and is usually accepting of anything enjoyable and fun. With Air, you have a fun and exciting relationship that will always give you something fresh and new. Air is always ready to enjoy fun with the one they love.

Strategy

The Air husband that you have may make you wonder why he dresses in suits or a sports coat to go to the grocery store. You may wonder why he talks so freely and jokes with people he doesn't even know. Your husband is full of life, love, and laughter. He only wants to share his joy for life with others because that's who he is, a breath of fresh air to everyone he meets. That is one of the first things you noticed and liked about him. He is still this way, but you are the one that has caught his eye and his heart.

You don't need to worry. What he needs from you is a playmate that will have fun, or make things fun, while keeping him grounded to the earth. He needs balance. To him, acceptance and affirmation mean a lot. His heart rejoices in fun but is comforted by everything being in order. In order, he can relax and enjoy the moment rather than panic. Since Air has no problems with physical or emotional intimacy, you can maintain the fun by being his playmate, confidant, and a reminder that being grounded to earth is a safe place to be.

~

Fire Strengths

When it comes to intimacy, Fire has to slow down a little, okay – a lot. Since Fire is always busy, he never feels he has enough time to complete all that he wants to do. This sometimes also includes you in that category. Because he is a very passionate person, his feelings run deep even though he can be selective in what he will allow himself to feel. For him, it's about what the moment and task call for. At the drop of a hat, he is prepared to move mountains. Just as quickly, he is prepared emotionally and mentally to move whatever mountains he must. Understand, your Fire husband is well equipped to perform wonders. If he sees the vision, he will develop the reasons, desires, and passion for making it happen. And when he says he will make it happen or do what he has to, he will.

In intimacy, this power translates into a deep and powerful passion. The only trick is to get the Fire to stop burning on a task, project, or his crusade to save the world long enough to burn in your direction.

The Fire husband has a short fuse when it comes to igniting his passion for intimacy. Just as quickly as he can be motivated to take on a project or the world, he could be equally as quick to come knocking on your door.

In Intimacy

Fire lives in a world of conviction, reason, and passion. Think of this as him having his own "Air" supply, which feeds his internal flame. Fire considers Air Personalities to be a slice of heaven because they are equally engaging, passionate, and inspirational. Fire needs these ingredients to remain passionate. These passions are just as powerful as he is and can sway him in one direction or another. As powerful as Fire is, he lives or dies by the amount of "Air" his mate has. His passions may be many. He is able to remain moral and upright as long as he doesn't develop a mindset where the "ends justify the means." In other words, if he can continue to resist getting what he wants at the risk of hurting others, he is able to remain pure.

This is important when it comes to intimacy. Why? The Fire Personality's power and strength are controlled by his convictions, emotions, and reasoning. For instance, if he is not being authentic because he's "doing what he has to" to get what he needs, then true intimacy will not be an option. However, if you tap into his inner core and learn the emotional being that lives there, respond to him as such, and he's yours as long as you remain true.

Fire personalities have a respect for words and the languages that use them. They are usually good communicators and can be quite convincing. This means they make great romance partners. Because they live in the world of passion and emotion, they really know how to captivate the heart (when they want to).

You never know when a Fire type will say something that hits you right in the heart. They can be just as emotionally powerful as they are effective.

Sex

As you might imagine, the power and strength of his ability to make things happen give him the determination to be a great partner both physically and emotionally. Sexually, he is given to spontaneity and may get "turned on" at the drop of a hat. He may prefer quick sessions that relieve unwanted stress and tension. For him, there doesn't have to be a special reason or moment. If he is convinced the timing is right, then he is ready for marital intimacy. Because his world is one of domination and controlling things, he may revert to a more passive lover, allowing you to take the lead. This also serves him because he wants to accomplish the task of pleasing you.

Each of the personality types has a second element or combination. The passion and desire of a Fire Personality will be adjusted accordingly. For element combinations, you may want to review them in *Mastering Your Personality,* Volumes One and Two. If not, there is enough information here to get a decent understanding. That being said, if your husband is a pure Fire husband (meaning he doesn't have a second or third combination to his personality like 'Fire-Water, or Fire-Air,' etc.), then he may want to fully control the intimate moment as well. A pure Fire husband has no problem telling you exactly what he wants in the bedroom.

Strategy

I heard it said that if a man is in love with the body of a woman, then any body will do. However, if he has learned to love the soul of his woman, then only she will do. You want to deepen the connection you have with him by touching the "Air" in him. Think of his Fire as the result of "Air" working in him. Take away his emotion, passion, visions, and dreams of the future, and he becomes frustrated and ineffective. He is results-oriented and does appreciate progress. But remember, his desired progress is only wanted because of his desires, visions, and dreams. Connect with him deeper by having intimate conversations with him about his passions and desires as they relate to what he wants in life, who he really is inside, and his vision for himself and his family. Throw in a little fiery boldness and say something sexy that he doesn't expect, and the intimacy game is on.

~

Water Strengths

It is not uncommon for the Water Personality to continue in their normal, mildly happy routine and suddenly be shocked by a request for verbal or physical intimacy. Because they have a general desire for things to be okay and good for everyone, they want to keep things "okay," and so they comply. As the conversation continues and things begin to progress, Water begins to feel a little uncomfortable. For Water, method and consistency are important. The conversation leading to verbal or physical intimacy isn't welcome. Water wants to continue in its path of the predictable.

Water wants any conversation of a serious nature to be slow and non-offensive. Intimacy in communication is important, but not as important as honesty and trustworthiness. Water not only looks at what is being said but the way it is being said. More sensitive to body language and changes in vocal tones, Water feels what is being communicated. Intimacy allows Water to listen and decide if the train of thought is fitting for the moment. To Water, the intimate conversation begins long before you say, "I want to talk..." Water looks at the pattern of conversations and your normal way of communicating things. Water is convinced of your love and dedication by what you continually say and not what you say in the heat of the moment. This is why they can overlook a few things said in the heat of an argument. The only problem with this is, if you consistently insult, belittle, or say the wrong thing, it becomes established as truth.

In Intimacy

Water is pleased to feel the love and warmth that is provided. Warmth and gentleness must accompany any desire that will become physical. Water doesn't like any sudden rushing when it comes to verbal or physical intimacy. Again, think of the Water Personality as a great body of water that you have to move by yourself. If you are going to be successful, you have to be very slow and methodical. With the Water Personality, patience rules. You can't just move Water the way you want without causing damage. Water never wants to be moved suddenly.

Intimacy has to be planned and prepared for. This is why physical intimacy usually is a planned activity that is part of a special occasion like a birthday, anniversary, or even a holiday. The Water Personality likes to take his time and enjoy the experience, especially because it may be a while before it comes around again.

Sex

Water has no problem with the planned and expected moment of physical intimacy. As in their normal everyday life, "How may I help you..."

becomes the question to answer. Water enjoys the experience but doesn't mind being there for the other person. Your Water husband is pleased with the opportunity to please you. On the other hand, Water may be reluctant to tell you what they want or even expect in the moment of physical intimacy. Just like the Water Personality can lead when given the proper tools and information, the same applies in the bedroom. Don't expect the Water Personality to just swing from the chandelier with spontaneity and creativity. They are dependable and consistent and can be easily accommodated.

Strategy

With the Water Personality, sex is like a mortgage payment; it should come once a month and keep you living comfortably for a while. To the other personality types (except Earth), that simply won't do. Water may want physical intimacy more than usual if there is a secondary personality type. Find out what your Water husband's second personality type is and play to that. As a Water Personality, intimacy must be planned out and taken slowly and methodically. Don't rush. If you rush Water, you ruin the moment and maybe even more moments to come. Realize that you have a gentle and faithful partner that loves to help, even with intimacy. Water needs you to want them enough to plan for it, not just spring it on them. Take your time and be patient. Speak with your Water husband and find out not only what he likes and wants, but more importantly, what turns him on.

Take a Moment

When you are intimate with your husband, are you wishing it was over or letting your mind wander to think of someone else? Is your sexuality about you, or does it include him too?

1) If you feel proud that you have let him know what you will and won't do in the bedroom, it has probably only been about you. Sure, some things are off-limits like sex with animals. Please remember for everything you say you won't do, five women are hinting or begging that they will do it for him. Sexually, you only have each other to meet needs. Why should you be the only one to get what you want the way you want it? Isn't he worth pleasing?

2) If you haven't studied him to know what he likes and when he likes it, you should spend more time in foreplay with him. Chances are, even though it's been a while, you may be simply tolerating some things he does in bed, or even the whole experience. You need to talk. If there is anything that you have experienced sexually with anyone else and enjoyed, you should now be doing that with your husband. Whatever you need from him, communicate it,

and he will comply. He only wants to please you, so help him.

Chapter 6
Loving Your Husband Without the But

> "Love your spouse more than you love your career, hobbies, and money. That stuff can never love you back anyway."
> **- Unknown**

When you consider the interesting mix of personalities within one person, you could find a world of mystery in every person you meet. For instance, it is not uncommon to find a Fire-Water personality type where the coping and harmony producing skills and habits are built automatically into the person's way of thinking and living. However, when it comes to putting a Fire personality type with a Water personality type, things may not flow as smoothly.

Why is that? One reason is that we have lost the ability to communicate with each other on a deeper level, a level that gets to the heart of the person and the heart of the matter. I am talking about a level of communication that is love-based, heartfelt, and truly nurturing. I am not talking about a communication that blames the other person or justifies another. I'm talking about truth that deepens our understanding and love for each other.

For reasons that I just mentioned, I've seen many things in relationships: like a Water person that can't get along with their Earth-Water mate even though it was the Water in them that attracted them to each other. You would think the Water personality would have common ground to stand on and mend any issues within the relationship. It didn't work at first for a very strong reason: communication.

Communication

As we look at the links of this chain, communication is first and should never be forgotten or neglected. Couples often skip communicating with each other for the sake of keeping the peace, saving time, or just not wanting to open a can of worms. I've found that not to communicate makes peace impossible, kills a lot of time, and turns a can of worms into a barrel of snakes. In other words, it makes things a lot worse.

Take A Moment

Consider the following areas of your communication about your relationship and your partner.

1) You have unspoken desires, frustrations, and issues with your husband that must be ironed out if you intend to find and keep happiness in your marriage relationship.

2) What you say to your girlfriends should be easily said to your husband. He should be your best friend and communicated with more intimately than your girlfriends. If you are speaking more truthfully to them than your husband, you are more intimate with your girlfriends than your own spouse. Don't let it happen, or don't let it continue.
3) The only way to cross this bridge of communication is to start opening your mouth, lovingly but truthfully, always being true to who you are.

Fear

Somewhere along the way, we have been made to feel afraid to show who we really are. This includes showing others our secrets. If they knew we liked a certain thing or desired a certain thing, they wouldn't like us. Because we value affirmation more than direction, we put on the mask to be liked by others – including our mates.

Take a Moment

Consider embracing the following suggestions around fear.

1) Gently but boldly walk away from your fear of being rejected by the one you married – be yourself without apology.

2) Stop being afraid of your husband's differences and find a place for every attribute and habit your husband has. There is a place for them in your life and purpose. Find a place for the things you don't like about your husband after you've understood the purpose for those things in his life.
3) Lovingly communicate what you need and stop being afraid to hurt his feelings. He can take it if you tell him in love.
4) Stop being afraid he will leave you or not love you anymore. I have found that heart to heart conversations create more love and trust. I've seen people get closer and not farther apart through loving conversation.

Married and Settling
If you are married and feel things won't get any better regardless of what you do, then you are suggesting marriage doesn't work and that it's better to live in a lie than to live the truth. This isn't true, and you don't have to settle.

Take a Moment

Be honest with yourself, do you want to live a life of settling? You don't have to.

1) All the reasons you fell in love with your husband still exist. The only thing is you've had a lot more of it, so it feels familiar. Take

the list of reasons you fell in love with your husband from the earlier chapters and go out on a date with your husband. Purposely focus on and appreciate those things.

2) Find out something new about your husband each month or week and add that to what you didn't know. Such conversations can start by you asking questions like, "What was your most embarrassing moment, happy moment, craziest thing you ever did?" etc.

3) Find something to compliment him on every single day.

4) Try to thank him more often.

5) Try to see things from his perspective before opening your mouth to say one word.

6) Set out to participate with him in his "moments" where he's doing something that annoys you.

7) Lastly, realize that every part of him was made for you and that there is something in his every action for you.

This last chapter included observations for you to take a moment and consider. I wanted to be intentional with encouraging you to learn to love what you hate about your mate. In this book, I have uncovered and dug into the depths of your personality and your husband's personality. I have sought to draw you closer through deeper communication, understanding, and even helping you to see that he is all you really need. Everything that you want in a man is there. The way you access the treasures is to understand his personality and work with him. You will never get what you are after by fighting him for it. You need to work with, not against him.

Finally, one of the greatest gifts this book offers is the chance to see him in a "new" light. He isn't the same old man, husband, or guy. He is a living, breathing, endless source of life, love, and adventure. He has so much more waiting for you to draw out of him.

Through the content of this book, the questions, and the opportunities included for you to pause and take a moment, you are well on your way to a deeper and more loving relationship than before. I wrote this book with both you and your husband in mind. So relax, if you guys are in this together, he's learning more about you, too. The love you've always wanted is the love you can have. While it may not happen overnight, that's okay – you have a lifetime together to experience it.

Love your husband without the but.

Next Steps

For coaching or to connect with Robert Pyles, visit rpthebig6.com

You may also invite Robert Pyles to speak by sending an email to pastorpyles@yourabundantfaith.org

Other Titles by Robert Pyles
Anchoring the Big 6

With over 20 years of experience as an Executive Coach, I've found that there are six primary areas in life that one must be anchored to experience exponential success in every area of their life. The Big 6 is not theory; it consists of proven principles to transform your life in Finance, Health, Relationships, Personal Development, Spiritual Growth, and Purpose. Before you make your next move, make sure you have mastered Anchoring The Big 6.

Coming Fall 2020
Mastering Your Personality Vol. I & II

www.ingramcontent.com/pod-product-compliance
Lightning Source LLC
Chambersburg PA
CBHW062033120526
44592CB00036B/2052